Royal Bank of Scotland

Warrants of the Charter

Erecting, confirming and granting new Privileges to the Royal Bank of Scotland

Royal Bank of Scotland

Warrants of the Charter
Erecting, confirming and granting new Privileges to the Royal Bank of Scotland

ISBN/EAN: 9783337039059

Printed in Europe, USA, Canada, Australia, Japan

Cover: Foto ©ninafisch / pixelio.de

More available books at **www.hansebooks.com**

WARRANTS

OF

THE CHARTER

ERECTING,

CONFIRMING AND GRANTING

NEW PRIVILEGES

TO THE

ROYAL BANK

OF

SCOTLAND.

𝕰𝖉𝖎𝖓𝖇𝖚𝖗𝖌𝖍:
PRINTED BY DAVID RAMSAY.
MDCCLXXXIX.

FIRST

WARRANT

OF

THE CHARTER

ERECTING THE

Royal Bank of Scotland.

∴⋯⋯∴⋯⋯∴

OUR SOVEREIGN LORD confidering, That, by an Act of Parliament made and paffed in the fifth year of his Majefty's reign, entitled, *An Act for fettling certain yearly funds, payable out of the Revenues of* Scotland, *to fatisfy public Debts in* Scotland, *and other ufes mentioned in the Treaty of Union; and to difcharge the Equivalents claimed on behalf of* Scotland, *in the terms of the fame Treaty; and for obviating all future difputes, charges, and expences con-* cerning

Preamble.

A

[2]

FIRST WARRANT.

Reciting the act of Parliament 1719, concerning the L.10,000 Annuity payable to the Creditors of the Public in Scotland,

cerning thefe Equivalents; it is enacted, amongſt other things, That yearly, and every year, from the Feaſt of the Nativity of St John the Baptiſt, one thouſand ſeven hundred and nineteen years, the full ſum of Ten thouſand pounds of lawful money of Great Britain ſhall be a yearly Fund for the particular purpoſes in that act expreſſed concerning the ſame; and ſhall continue and be payable for ever, ſubject, neverthelefs, to redemption by Parliament, according to a *proviſo* in the ſaid act contained in that behalf; and that the ſaid annuity of Ten thouſand pounds, during the continuance thereof, ſhall be charged and chargeable upon, and be payable and paid out of the

out of the Cuſtoms and Excife, and other duties, under the management of the Commiſſioners of theſe revenues in Scotland.

monies ariſen and to arife, from time to time, of or from any the cuſtoms, duties, excifes, or revenues, that are or ſhall be under the management of the Commiſſioners of the Cuſtoms and Commiſſioners of Excife in Scotland,

or

or of any Commiffioners, Farmers, or Managers of thofe revenues, or either of them, for the time being, with fuch preference, as in the faid act is mentioned; which faid annuity is thereby enacted to be payable quarterly, in manner in the faid act mentioned, and to be free from all taxes and impofitions whatfoever, laid or to be laid thereupon, by authority of Parliament. And it is thereby further enacted, That it fhould and might be lawful to and for his Majefty, by letters patent under the Great Seal of Great Britain, to incorporate all and every the Proprietors of the debts and fums of money, ftated to amount to the principal fum of Two hundred and thirty thoufand three hundred and eight pounds nine fhillings ten pence and five fixth parts of a penny, due to the creditors of the public in Scotland, on the twenty-fourth day of June one thoufand feven hundred and fourteen years, and

Eighteen

FIRST WARRANT.

Free from all taxes and impofitions whatfoever.

His Majefty authorifed to incorporate the Proprietors of the debts ftated to amount to L.248,550 : 0 : 9½,

due to the creditors of the public in Scotland.

FIRST
WARRANT.

By such name as
he should think fit.

And the said
L.248,550:0:9½,
should be the Ca-
pital or Joint Stock
of the Corporation,

Eighteen thousand two hundred and forty-one pounds ten shillings ten pence and two thirds of a penny, stated due to William Paterson, Esq. making together Two hundred and forty-eight thousand five hundred and fifty pounds and nine pence halfpenny, to be one Body Politic and Corporate, by such name as his Majesty should think most proper, and that by such name the said Corporation should have perpetual succession, subject to such redemption, as in the said act is appointed: With such powers to do and perform all matters appertaining to them to do and perform, touching or concerning the said capital sums, and the said yearly fund payable in respect thereof, as his Majesty by the same letters patent should think fit to grant. And it was thereby enacted, That the said capital sum, amounting to Two hundred forty-eight thousand five hundred and fifty pounds

[5]

pounds and nine pence halfpenny, should be, and be deemed to be, the Capital or Joint Stock of the said Corporation; and that the shares of the Members of and in the same should be from time to time assignable, transferable, and deviseable, in such manner as his Majesty by such letters patent should prescribe and appoint, until the redemption thereof; and that the same should be deemed to be personal or moveable estates, and should go to executors or administrators, and should not be liable to any arrestments or attachments that should be laid thereupon. And it is thereby enacted, That all and every the Members of the said Corporation should have and be entitled to an annuity or yearly sum, in proportion to his or their share in the said capital sum and stock of Two hundred and forty-eight thousand five hundred and fifty pounds and nine pence halfpenny; and the said

FIRST WARRANT.

And be deemed personal or moveable estates,

not liable to arrestments or attachments.

FIRST WARRANT.

L. 600 per annum to be paid to the Corporation for charges of management.

Recital of the charter erecting the Proprietors of the foresaid debt into a Corporation, by the name of the EQUIVALENT COMPANY.

said annuity should be paid in the manner in the said act mentioned, and to and for no other use, intent, or purpose whatsoever. And it was further enacted, That, above the said annuity of Ten thousand pounds per annum, there should be paid to the said Corporation and their successors, until the redemption of such annual sum, the further annual sum of Six hundred pounds per annum, towards the necessary charges of the management thereof, as in and by the said act of Parliament, amongst other clauses and things therein contained, relation being thereunto had, doth and may more fully and at large appear. And considering, That his Majesty, by his letters patent, bearing date at Westminster, the twenty-first day of November, in the eleventh year of his reign, in pursuance of the said act of Parliament, and by virtue of his prerogative royal, and likewise of his especial grace,

grace, certain knowledge, and mere motion, did give, grant, make, ordain, declare, appoint, and establish, That all and every person or persons, natives and foreigners, bodies politic and corporate, who then were Proprietors of the debts and sums of money so stated to amount to Two hundred forty-eight thousand five hundred fifty pounds and nine pence halfpenny, or who, by any lawful title, derived, or to be derived, from, by, or under the said Proprietors at any time thereafter, should have, or be entitled to any part, share, or interest therein, should be, and be called, one Body Politic and Corporate of themselves, in deed and name, by the name of the EQUIVALENT COMPANY; and that such Corporation, and their successors, should have perpetual succession, subject to such redemption as is therein mentioned; and should and might have and use a common seal, and should,

FIRST WARRANT.

FIRST WARRANT.

should, by that name, be capable to sue and be sued; and that the sum of Two hundred forty-eight thousand five hundred and fifty pounds and nine pence halfpenny, should be accepted, deemed, and esteemed the Capital or Joint Stock of the said Corporation, and all the Proprietors of such stock should be Members of the said Corporation; and that the said annuity of Ten thousand pounds per annum should be paid to the said Company or their Cashier, to be divided and distributed to and amongst the several Proprietors, in proportion to their respective shares in the said Capital or Joint Stock. And his Majesty did thereby further order and direct, limit, and appoint, That the said stock should be transferable and assignable; and all assignments and transfers of the said capital stock, or yearly fund, or any part thereof, should be in the manner, and according to the methods thereby

The foresaid L.248,550 : 0 : 9½ to be the Capital or Joint Stock of the EQUIVALENT COMPANY.

And the annuity of L.10,000, payable to the Company or their Cashier, to be divided amongst the Proprietors, according to their shares in the stock.

The stock of the Company to be transferable.

thereby directed: And likewife appointed, That the faid annual fum of Six hundred pounds for charges of management, fhould be paid to the faid Corporation, or fuch as they fhould authorife, under their common feal, to receive the fame, for the ufes of the faid Corporation. And whereas many of the Proprietors of the faid ftock refided in England, and others in Scotland, who might be defirous to have their intereft in the faid annual and capital fums paid and fecured either in London or Edinburgh, according to the place of their refpective refidence; his Majefty did ordain and appoint, That all and every perfon and perfons interefted in the debentures therein mentioned, fhould and might, at the time of their delivering up the faid debentures to the faid Corporation, declare at which of the faid places he or they would have his or their fhare or intereft in the faid annual and

<small>FIRST WARRANT.

The L. 600 is payable to the EQUIVALENT COMPANY, or any perfon to be appointed by them, under their feal, to receive the fame.</small>

B capital

FIRST WARRANT.

Diſtinct books of ſubſcription to be kept at London and Edinburgh, wherein the Proprietors are to declare at which of theſe places they are to have credit for their ſtock.

Diſtinct books of transfer to be kept at theſe places likewiſe.

Two of the Directors to be for ever choſen, reſiding at Edinburgh, to have the cuſtody of theſe books.

capital ſums paid and ſecured; and, according to ſuch declaration, each reſpective Proprietor ſhould have credit in diſtinct books to be kept at London and Edinburgh for that purpoſe, and receive their ſhares and proportions of the ſaid annual and capital ſums, when redeemed, at London or Edinburgh, according to their reſpective credits in the ſaid ſeparate and diſtinct books; and that diſtinct and ſeparate books ſhould be kept at London and Edinburgh for transferring the ſhares, credits, and intereſts of the reſpective Proprietors, according to their reſpective intereſts therein, in ſuch manner and form as is therein directed and appointed. And that for the better conduct and management of this affair at Edinburgh, there ſhould be for ever choſen, until redemption as aforeſaid, at leaſt two of the thirteen Directors to reſide and be at Edinburgh, who ſhould have the cuſtody, dy, care, and management of the several and respective books at Edinburgh, under such rules, orders, and directions, as they should, from time to time, receive from the said Court of Directors of the said Corporation. Provided always, that, as often as any of the share or shares, or interest of any person or persons who should have credit in the books kept at Edinburgh, should be purchased by any person or persons residing at London, or the share or shares, or interest of any person or persons who should have credit in the books kept at London, should be purchased by any person or persons at Edinburgh, the same might be discharged in one book, and new credit taken in the other respectively, as the person or persons entitled to the same should desire or require the same. And his Majesty did thereby for himself, his heirs, and successors, covenant, grant, and agree to and with the said Corporation

FIRST WARRANT.

Stock in the books at London may be discharged therefrom, and new credit got in the books at Edinburgh, and reciprocally for stock at Edinburgh.

His Majesty covenants to give the EQUIVALENT COMPANY further powers and privileges upon their humble suit and request.

[12]

FIRST WARRANT.

Corporation or Body Politic, and their fucceffors, that he, his heirs, and fucceffors, fhould, from time to time, and at all times thereafter, upon the humble fuit and requeft of the faid Corporation or Body Politic, and their fucceffors, give and grant unto them all fuch further and other powers, privileges, and authorities, matters, and things, for rendering more effectual their faid grant, according to the true intent and meaning of the faid act, and of the faid grant, which he could or might lawfully grant, fubject to the power of redemption therein mentioned, as by the faid grant or letters patent paffed under the Great Seal of Great Britain, relation being thereunto had, doth and may more fully and at large appear. And confidering that the faid Corporation have, by their moft humble application to his Majefty, requefted, That he would be gracioufly pleafed, by letters patent under the

Recital of the petition of the EQUIVALENT COMPANY for obtaining a power of Banking, &c. in Scotland.

the Great Seal of Scotland, to enable such of the Proprietors of the said Corporation as should subscribe their stock for that purpose, to have the power of Banking in Scotland only, with liberty to borrow and lend upon security there; that the said Corporation may be for that purpose impowered to take subscriptions at Edinburgh from their Members, for such share of the stock as they shall incline to subject to such Trade or Banking, under such regulations as they by byelaws shall appoint; and that such subscribed stock only shall be affected by the transactions relating to Banking, and shall (after being so subscribed) become transferable from the other stock of the Company, and at Edinburgh only; and would erect such subscribers into a Corporation for that purpose, and that such power of Banking so established, would manifestly tend to the great benefit and advantage

FIRST WARRANT.

To such of their Members as should subscribe all or part of their stock, into the books of subscription to be opened at Edinburgh.

Such subscribed stock only to be subject to the transactions of Banking, and thereafter to be transferable from the other stock of the Equivalent Company, and at Edinburgh only.

FIRST WARRANT.

tage of that part of his kingdom; and his Majesty being willing to give all proper encouragements to such an undertaking, therefore his Majesty, in compliance with the said request, and by virtue of his prerogative royal, and of his especial grace, certain knowledge, and mere motion, and for the benefit of his subjects in that part of his united kingdoms, ordains a Charter to be made and passed under the Seal appointed by the Treaty of Union to be kept in Scotland, in place of the Great Seal thereof, nominating, authorising, and appointing, as his Majesty by these presents nominates, authorises, and appoints James Campbell, Paul D'Aranda, John Drummond, Edward Harrison, Daniel Hays, Benjamin Longuet, John Merill, Bulstrode Peachy Knight, Christopher Tilson, Robert Williamson, Esqrs. Sir Hew Dalrymple, Bart. Lord President of the Session, Patrick Campbell of Monzie,

A Charter ordained to pass the Seal of Scotland,

authorising the Directors of the EQUIVALENT COMPANY, or any three of them, in such way as the majority of them shall direct,

zie, and Patrick Crawford, Esqrs. or any three of them, in such way and manner as they, or the majority of them, shall direct, to take and receive at Edinburgh, all such voluntary subscriptions as shall be made, on or before the twenty-ninth day of September one thousand seven hundred and twenty-seven years, by any person or persons, Members or Proprietors of the said Equivalent Company, who have, or shall have credit for stock in the books of the said Company at Edinburgh, at the time of such subscription, of all or any of such part or share of the stock of the said Equivalent Company, as he, she, or they, shall think proper, for and towards raising a fund for the more effectually carrying on the said trade and business of Banking there, and the uses herein after mentioned; which said subscriptions, the said Proprietors are hereby impowered to make, and the same shall

FIRST WARRANT.

to receive at Edinburgh all such voluntary subscriptions, as should be made on or before the 29th of September 1727, by the Proprietors of the said Company, who shall, at subscribing, have credit for stock in the Company's books at Edinburgh.

FIRST WARRANT.

Which subscriptions are to be entered in books to be kept for that purpose.

The stock so subscribed, to be under the management of the Company hereby established.

shall be fairly entered in books to be kept for that purpose, and the present stock of the said Equivalent Company, so to be subscribed as aforesaid, shall, from and after the time of such subscription, be under the order, management, and direction of the Company hereby established. And his Majesty, by virtue of his said prerogative, and likewise of his especial grace, certain knowledge, and mere motion, hath given, granted, made, ordained, constituted, declared, appointed, and established, and by these presents, for himself, his heirs, and successors, gives, grants, makes, ordains, constitutes, declares, appoints, and establishes, That all and every person or persons, natives and foreigners, bodies politic and corporate, Proprietors of the said stock, who shall subscribe any share or shares of the said stock, and who, as executors, administrators, successors, or assignees, or by any other lawful title,

to

[17]

to be derived from, by, or under the said subscribers, at any time or times hereafter, shall have or be entitled to any part, share, or interest of or in the said stock, so to be subscribed as aforesaid, shall be and be called one Body Politic and Corporate of themselves, in deed and name, by the name of *The Royal Bank of Scotland;* and that such Corporation, and their successors, by the said name, shall have perpetual succession, and shall and may have and use a common seal, and that they and their successors, by the same name, shall be able and capable in law to sue and implead, pursue and defend, be sued and impleaded, pursued and defended, answer and be answered, in all or any of his Majesty's Courts within Scotland; and that they and their successors, by the name aforesaid, shall and may be able and capable in law to have, purchase, receive, possess, enjoy, and retain to them and their successors,

FIRST WARRANT.

The subscribers to be called by the name of *The Royal Bank of Scotland*, and by that name to have perpetual succession,

and a common seal, &c. be capable in law to sue and be sued, &c. in any of the Courts within Scotland.

C

[18]

FIRST WARRANT.

To purchafe lands, &c. in Scotland,

and to fell the fame.

The *Royal Bank* to have a power of Banking within Scotland.

To lend any fums at any intereft not exceeding lawful intereft upon perfonal and real fecurity, and pledges of any kind.

fors, lands, rents, tenements, and hereditaments, of what kind, nature, or quality foever, in Scotland only; and alfo to fell, grant, demife, analzie, or difpone the fame: And his Majefty doth hereby, for himfelf, his heirs, and fucceffors, grant unto the faid Company of the *Royal Bank of Scotland*, and their fucceffors for ever, full power and liberty to exercife the rights and powers of Banking, in that part of his united kingdom called Scotland only; and in particular to lend to any perfon or perfons, bodies politic or corporate, fuch fum and fums of money, as they fhall think fit, at any intereft not exceeding lawful intereft, on real or perfonal fecurity; and particularly on pledges of any kind whatfoever, of any goods, wares, merchandifes, or other effects whatfoever, in fuch way and manner as to the faid Company fhall feem proper and convenient; and that the faid Company

may

may keep the money or cash of any person or persons, bodies politic and corporate whatsoever, and may borrow, owe, or take up in Scotland, on their bills or notes payable on demand, to be signed in such manner, and by such persons, as the Court of Directors herein after-mentioned shall direct and appoint, or in such other manner as the said Court of Directors shall think fit, any sum or sums of money whatsoever. And his Majesty doth hereby declare, direct, and appoint, That the said Company shall not, at any time or times, deal or trade, or permit or suffer any person or persons whatsoever, either in trust or for the benefit of the same, to deal or trade with any of the stock, money, or effects, of or any ways belonging to the said Corporation, in the buying or selling of any goods, wares, or merchandises whatsoever; provided, that nothing herein contained shall any ways be

FIRST WARRANT.

The *Royal Bank* may keep the cash of other persons, and borrow, owe, and take up money on their bills or notes payable on demand.

A prohibition to trade with the money or stock of the Company, in buying or selling wares of any sort.

Allowance nevertheless to deal in bills of exchange, in buying bullion, &c.

FIRST WARRANT.

And selling wares *bona fide* pledged,

and lands, &c. purchased, and the produce thereof.

be construed to extend to hinder the said Corporation from dealing in bills of exchange, or in buying or selling bullion, gold, or silver in Scotland only, or extend to hinder the said Corporation from selling any goods, wares, merchandises, or effects whatsoever, which shall really and *bona fide* be pledged, left, or deposited with the said Corporation, for money lent and advanced thereon, and which shall not be redeemed at the time agreed on, or from selling such lands, rents, tenements, or hereditaments, as they shall purchase, in virtue of the power aforesaid, or from selling such goods as shall or may be the produce of lands purchased by the said Corporation. And for the better accomplishment of the ends and intentions proposed by the erecting of the said Corporation, and for making and establishing a continual succession of fit persons to be the Managers and Directors of the said Corporation,

[21]

Corporation, his Majesty doth, by these presents, for himself, his heirs, and successors, grant unto the said *Royal Bank of Scotland*, and to their successors, and doth hereby ordain and appoint, That there shall be, from time to time, a Governor, Deputy-Governor, nine Ordinary Directors, and nine Extraordinary Directors, to be chosen out of the Members of the said Company; which said Governor, Deputy-Governor, and nine Ordinary Directors, or any five or more of them, shall be and be called *A Court of Directors*, for ordering, managing, and directing all the affairs of the said Corporation, in manner by these presents mentioned; and that our right trusty and right well-beloved cousin and counsellor Archibald Earl of Ilay, shall be the present and first Governor, and Sir Hew Dalrymple, Lord President of our Session, the present and first Deputy-Governor, and Andrew Fletcher, Esq. one

of

FIRST WARRANT.

That there shall be, from time to time, a Governor, Deputy-Governor, nine Ordinary, & nine Extraordinary Directors, for managing the affairs of the Corporation. The Governor, Deputy-Governor, and nine Ordinary Directors, or any five of them, to be called *A Court of Directors*.

The names of the first Governor, Deputy-Governor, and Directors;

FIRST WARRANT.

of the Senators of the College of Juſtice, George Drummond, Eſq. Lord Provoſt of Edinburgh, Patrick Campbell of Monzie, Eſq. Richard Dowdeſwell, Eſq. John Philp, Eſq. James Paterſon, Eſq. one of the Commiſſaries of Edinburgh, Hugh Somervell, Eſq. writer to the ſignet, Patrick Crawfurd, ſen. Eſq. George Irving, of Newton, Eſq. the preſent and nine firſt Ordinary Directors; and Matthew Lant, Chief Baron of our Court of Exchequer in Scotland, James Erſkine, Eſq. one of the Senators of the College of Juſtice, Sir John Clerk, one of the Barons of our ſaid Court of Exchequer, Hew Dalrymple, Eſq. one of the Senators of the College of Juſtice, George Baillie, of Jerviſwood, Eſq. Charles Cathcart, Eſq. our Receiver-General for Scotland, George Roſs, Eſq. one of our Commiſſioners of Exciſe in Scotland, Charles Areſkine, Eſq. our Solicitor-General for Scotland, and

James

James Nimmo, Esq. Cashier to our Commissioners of Excise in Scotland, the present and first nine Extraordinary Directors; and shall continue in their respective offices, until the twenty-fourth day of December, which shall be in the year one thousand seven hundred and twenty-eight, and till others shall be duly chosen into their respective offices, and sworn into the same, unless they, or any of them, shall sooner die, or be removed, as is herein after mentioned. And his Majesty doth hereby, for himself, his heirs, and successors, give and grant to the said Corporation hereby established, and their successors, and he doth hereby will and appoint, That it shall and may be lawful to and for all and every the Members of the said Corporation or Body Politic hereby established, from time to time, to assemble and meet together, at any convenient place or places in Edinburgh, for the choice

FIRST WARRANT.

who are to continue till Christmas 1728, and till others are chosen, and sworn into their places.

The Members of the Corporation may, from time to time, meet at Edinburgh, for chusing of their Governor, Deputy-Governor, and Directors;

choice of their Governor, Deputy-Governor, and Directors, and for making of by-laws, ordinances, rules, orders, and directions, for the government of the said Corporation; public notice thereof being first given in the Edinburgh Courant, and in writing to be affixed on the market-crofs of Edinburgh, thirty days at least before the time appointed for such meeting; and that all the Members of the said Corporation hereby established, or so many of them as shall be assembled, shall be and be called *A General Court* of the said Corporation: Which Courts shall meet and assemble at such time, and in such manner as are herein after directed. And his Majesty doth hereby direct, That there shall be held four General Courts of the Proprietors of the said Company in every year, on the days and at the times following, that is to say, on the last Tuesday of the month of November, on the first

Tuesday

FIRST WARRANT.

and for making by-laws, &c.

Public notice thereof to be given thirty days at least before the time appointed for such meeting.

The Members so assembled to be called *A General Court* of the Corporation.

Tuesday in the month of March, on the first Tuesday in the month of June; and the first Tuesday in the month of September every year; and that all succeeding Governors, Deputy-Governors, and Directors of the said Corporation, shall, from and after the said twenty-fourth day of December one thousand seven hundred and twenty-eight years, be every year chosen for ever out of the Members of the said Corporation (the said Governor then having in his own right Two thousand pounds or more of the Capital Stock of the said Company, the said Deputy-Governor then having in his own right One thousand five hundred pounds or more of the Capital Stock of the said Company, the said nine Ordinary Directors then having each of them respectively One thousand pounds or more of the Capital Stock of the said Company, and the said nine Extraordinary Directors then having each

FIRST WARRANT.

That there be four General Courts in the year.

The Governor, Deputy-Governor, and Directors, after the 24th December 1728, to be chosen annually on the 1st Tuesday of March.

Their qualifications of Stock, viz. the Governor, 2000l. Deputy-Governor, 1500l. an Ordinary Director, 1000l. an Extraordinary Director, 500l.

FIRST
WARRANT.

each of them respectively Five hundred pounds or more of the Capital Stock of the said Company), on the first Tuesday of March every year, by the majority of votes of all and every the Members of the said Corporation present at such General Court: Provided, That no person shall be capable to vote in such, or any other General Court, who shall not, at the time of such voting, appear to have Three hundred pounds or more of the Capital Stock of the said Corporation, in his, her, or their own name or names; and that every Member shall have one vote for Three hundred pounds, two votes for Six hundred pounds, three for One thousand two hundred pounds, and four for Two thousand pounds, of such Capital Stock, as he, she, or they, shall have in the said book or books, in his, her, or their own name or names; but no person shall have above four votes for or in respect of any sum whatsoever,

One vote allowed for 300l. two votes for 600l. three votes for 1200l. and four votes for 2000l.

No person entitled to more than four votes.

whatsoever, as he, she, or they shall have, as aforesaid; and in case of the absence of any of the said Proprietors, it shall and may be lawful for every such Proprietor, being absent, by writing under his hand, attested by two or more credible witnesses, to authorise and appoint any one of the Members of the said Corporation, having Three hundred pounds Stock at the least in his name, in the book or books of the said Corporation, to be his proxy, and give a vote or votes for him, and in his name, at any such General Court and Courts, in the election of Governor, Deputy-Governor, and Directors. And his Majesty doth hereby further direct, order, and appoint, That every person claiming a right to vote in any General Court or Courts of the said Company, shall, if desired and required by any other of the Proprietors duly qualified to vote at any such General Court, be obliged, and is hereby directed

FIRST WARRANT.

Proxies qualified with Stock, allowed to vote in elections.

[28]

FIRST WARRANT.

Form of the oath that may be put to persons claiming to vote,

to be administered by the Governor or Deputy-Governor, or, in their absence, by any two Directors.

No person refusing to take such oath, shall be capable to vote.

directed to take the corporal oath following, viz. *I* A. B. *do swear, that the sum of   of the Capital Stock of the Body Politic called* The Royal Bank of Scotland, *doth at this time belong to me in my own right, and not in trust for any person or persons whatsoever;* which said oath shall and may be administered by the Governor or Deputy-Governor of the said Company for the time being, or, in the absence of the said Governor and Deputy-Governor, then by any two of the Directors then present; and they are hereby respectively authorised to administer such oath to all and every person and persons claiming a right to vote in such General Courts from time to time accordingly, upon such desire and request, as aforesaid; and that no person refusing to take such oath, after being desired, as aforesaid, shall be capable to vote at such General Courts of the said Company: Provided always, That

[29]

That all and every the Proprietors of the said Company, who shall, at any time or times, authorise any other Proprietor to vote as a proxy for him in such General Courts, as aforesaid, shall make oath before one of his Majesty's Justices of the Peace, or the Chief Magistrate of any city or burgh, where such person resides, that the sum of   of the Capital Stock of the Body Politic, called *The Royal Bank of Scotland*, doth, at the time of his signing such authority, belong to him in his own right, and not in trust for any person or persons whatsoever, which said affidavit shall be produced by every person claiming a right to vote by proxy, as aforesaid; and no person or persons shall be allowed to vote as a proxy, as aforesaid, unless they not only produce the authority impowering him to vote as proxy, as aforesaid, but also such affidavit, so sworn by the person authorising him

to

FIRST WARRANT.

The same oath to be taken by such as appoint proxies before a Justice of Peace, or Chief Magistrate of a burgh.

The Proxy to produce his powers for voting, with such affidavit, to the General Court.

[30]

FIRST
WARRANT.

to vote as his proxy, as aforesaid. And his Majesty doth hereby further direct and appoint, That all succeeding Governors, Deputy-Governors, and Directors, so chosen, as aforesaid, shall severally and respectively continue in their respective offices, to which they shall be severally elected, for one year, and till others shall be duly chosen, and sworn into their places respectively. Provided nevertheless, That, in case of death, avoidance, or removal of the said Governor, Deputy-Governor, or any of the said Directors, for the time being, the survivors of them, or the majority of those remaining in their offices, shall and may at any time, upon such notice given, as aforesaid, assemble together the Members of the said Corporation at Edinburgh, in order to elect other persons, by Members qualified to vote in manner as aforesaid, in the room of those dead, removed, or whose places shall become void;

Each succeeding Governor, Deputy-Governor, and Directors, so chosen, to continue for one year, and till others are chosen and sworn into their places.

In case of the death, &c. of any of them, those remaining in their offices may call a General Court, to chuse others in their rooms.

void: Provided alſo, That no perſon ſhall be capable of being choſen Governor, Deputy-Governor, or Director of the ſaid Corporation, who ſhall not, at the time of ſuch choice, be a natural born ſubject of Great Britain, or naturalized; and ſuch Governor ſhall then alſo have in his own name, and for his own uſe, Two thouſand pounds or more of the ſaid Capital Stock, and ſuch Deputy-Governor ſhall then alſo have in his own name, and for his own uſe, Fifteen hundred pounds or more of the ſaid Capital Stock, and ſuch Ordinary Directors having each of them reſpectively in their own names, and for their own uſe, One thouſand pounds or more of the ſaid Capital Stock, and ſuch Extraordinary Directors having each of them reſpectively in their own name, and for their own uſe, Five hundred pounds or more of the ſaid Capital Stock; and that the ſaid Governor, Deputy-

FIRST WARRANT.

None to be choſen into theſe offices, but ſuch as are ſubjects of Great Britain, or naturalized, and qualified with ſtock, as aforeſaid.

FIRST WARRANT.

And not to continue in those offices longer than the continuance of stock in their own names and rights.

Deputy-Governor, or Directors, shall not continue in his or their respective offices longer than the continuance of such their respective interests and stocks in their own names and rights, and to their own uses respectively; but upon parting with, or reducing his or their respective share or interests in the said Capital Stock, to any lesser sum than as aforesaid, the said respective offices or places of such Governor, Deputy-Governor, or Directors, so parting with, reducing, or diminishing their said interests, as aforesaid, shall cease, determine, and become vacant, and others may be chosen in their rooms, by a General Court of the said Corporation, as aforesaid. Provided also, and his Majesty doth, by these presents, for himself, his heirs, and successors, will, ordain, and appoint, That none of the said persons hereby mentioned to be the first Governor, Deputy-Governor, and Directors,

tors of the said Corporation, or any other person or persons hereafter to be chosen to the office or trust of a Governor, Deputy-Governor, or Director of the said Corporation, shall be capable to execute or act in the said office and trust of a Governor, Deputy-Governor, or Director, at any time or times hereafter, until he or they shall respectively take the corporal oath following, viz. *I A. B. do swear, that the sum of   of the Capital Stock of the Body Politic called* The Royal Bank of Scotland, *whereof I am elected or appointed to be a   doth at this time belong to me, in my own right, and not in trust for any person or persons whatsoever.* And likewise another oath, in the form and to the effect following: *I A. B. do swear, that, in the office of   of* The Royal Bank of Scotland, *I will be indifferent and equal to all manner of persons, and I will give my best advice and assistance for*

FIRST WARRANT.

Nor shall they be capable to act till they have taken the oath of office.

Form of the oath.

E   the

FIRST WARRANT.

the *support and good government of the said Corporation; and, in the execution of the office of   , I will faithfully and honestly demean myself, according to the best of my skill and understanding. So help me God.* Which said oaths to the said present and future Governor, and Deputy-Governor and Directors, shall and may be administered by the Lord Chief Baron, or any of the Barons of the Court of Exchequer in Scotland of his Majesty, his heirs, and successors, for the time being, or by any two of the Directors, who shall have taken the oaths in manner aforesaid; and they are hereby respectively authorised to administer the said oaths to all and every such Governor, Deputy-Governor, Director, and Directors, from time to time, accordingly. And furthermore, his Majesty's will and pleasure is, and he doth hereby for himself, his heirs, and successors, ordain and appoint, that the

To be administered by any of the Barons of the Court of Exchequer, or any two Directors, who shall have taken the said oaths before any of the Barons of that Court.

the said Governor, Deputy-Governor, and Court of Directors, or any two of them, shall have power and authority to administer an oath to the Cashier, and all other the inferior agents or servants that shall be employed in the service of the said Company, for the faithful and due execution of the several places and trusts in them reposed. And it is hereby further provided and declared,— That no person nominated, or that shall hereafter be nominated or elected to the office of Governor, Deputy-Governor, or Director, or into the office of Cashier, or into any other inferior office in the service of the said Company, shall be capable to sit, vote, or act, or to exercise, use, and discharge any such office, until he shall first have produced before the Lord Chief Baron, or any other of the Barons of the Court of Exchequer in Scotland, or before the Court of Directors of the said Company, certificates from the proper

FIRST WARRANT.

An oath &c. shall to be administered to the Cashier and other officers.

No Governor, Deputy-Governor, or Director, nor any officer or servant under them, shall be capable to act, until such have produced certificates from the proper officers of their having taken the oaths to the Government.

FIRST WARRANT.

proper officers, of his having taken and subscribed the several oaths, which now are, or by any subsequent law, shall be directed to be taken by all persons bearing or holding any office, civil or military, under his Majesty, his heirs, and successors. And it is hereby further provided and declared, That, in case any person hereby nominated, or hereafter to be elected a Governor, Deputy-Governor, or Director, as aforesaid, shall, for the space of forty days after such nomination or election, if in Scotland, or for the space of forty days after they come into Scotland, neglect or refuse to take the said oaths hereby appointed to be by him taken, as aforesaid, or shall refuse or neglect to take upon him his office—that then, and in every such cases, the office or place of every such person so neglecting or refusing shall become vacant, and others may be chosen in their places by a General Court of the said

Any neglecting to take the said oaths, or to take upon them their office for forty days, if in Scotland, or forty days after their coming into Scotland, their places shall become vacant,

and others may be chosen in their places, by a General Court.

said Corporation, as aforesaid. And his Majesty doth, by these presents, will, direct, and appoint, That the said Governor, Deputy-Governor, and Court of Directors, for the time being, or the major part of them, which shall be present at any Court of Directors for the time being, may, as they shall see occasion, upon thirty days notice to be given, as aforesaid, summon and call a General Court of the said Company; and likewise shall, from time to time, upon demand to be made by any nine or more of the said Members, having each One thousand pounds, or more interest or share in the said Capital Stock, within thirty days after such demand, summon and call such General Court to be held at Edinburgh, of the Members of the said Corporation, qualified as aforesaid, and in default of the said Governor, Deputy-Governor, and Court of Directors, or the major part of them,

which

FIRST WARRANT.

The Court of Directors, or major part of them, may call a General Court, upon thirty days notice;

and shall, upon demand of any nine or more of the Members, having each 1000l. Stock, call a General Court.

FIRST
WARRANT.

And in their default of calling fuch Court, the faid nine or more Members, having each 1000l. Stock, may fummon and hold a General Court, upon notice as aforefaid;

which General Court, for any mifdemeanour or abufe, may remove or difplace the Governor, Deputy-Governor, or any of the Directors, and elect and chufe others in their rooms.

which fhall be prefent at any fuch Court, for the time being, to fummon and call fuch Court, it fhall and may be lawful to and for the faid nine or more Members, having each One thoufand pounds Stock, as aforefaid, or more, upon thirty days notice, to be given in the Edinburgh Courant, and in writing, to be affixed upon the market crofs of Edinburgh, to fummon and hold a General Court, and there to difpatch any bufinefs relating to the government or affairs of the faid Corporation, and to remove or difplace the faid Governor, Deputy-Governor, and any of the faid Directors, for any mifdemeanours, or abufe of his or their offices, and elect and chufe another or others, in his or their rooms, in the fame manner as the faid elections, on the firft Tuefday in March yearly, are herein before directed to be made; and in every cafe where the Governor, Deputy-Governor, or any Director

FIRST WARRANT.

tor or Directors, shall happen to die, or be removed, or whose office shall otherwise become void before the expiration of the time for which he shall have been elected, the major part of the Members of the said Corporation, to be assembled in a General Court at Edinburgh, being qualified as aforesaid, shall and may elect and chuse any other Member or Members of the said Corporation qualified for a Governor, Deputy-Governor, or Directors, as aforesaid, into the office of such Governor, Deputy-Governor, Director, or Directors, that shall so die or be removed, or whose offices shall so become void; which persons, so to be chosen, shall continue in the said office or offices until the next usual time hereby appointed for election, and till others shall be duly chosen and sworn. And, for the better managing and ordering the affairs of the said Corporation, his Majesty doth, by

these

[40]

FIRST WARRANT.

thefe prefents, for himfelf, his heirs, and fucceffors, grant unto the faid Body Politic, and their fucceffors for ever, and he doth, by thefe prefents, will and appoint, That the faid Governor, Deputy-Governor, and Ordinary Directors, for the time being, or any five or more of them, fhall and may, from time to time, and at all times, affemble and meet together, at any place or places in Edinburgh, for the direction and management of the affairs of the faid Corporation, and then and there to hold Courts for the purpofes aforefaid, and fummon General Courts to meet as aforefaid, as they fhall fee caufe; and the faid Governor, Deputy-Governor, and Directors, or the majority of them, fo affembled, fhall and may act, according to fuch by-laws, conftitutions, orders, rules, and directions, as fhall, from time to time, be lawfully made and given unto them by the General Court of

The Governor, Deputy-Governor, & Directors, or any five of them, may meet at any place in Edinburgh, for the management of the affairs of the Corporation,

and hold Courts, and fummon General Courts, as they fee caufe.

of the said Corporation, in purfuance of this his Majefty's Charter, and in all cafes where fuch by-laws, conftitutions, orders, rules, or directions, by or from the General Court, fhall be wanting, the faid Governor, Deputy-Governor, or Directors, or the major part of them fo affembled, fhall and may direct and manage all the affairs and bufinefs of the faid Corporation; and fhall and may appoint a Cafhier and Secretary, and all other agents or fervants, which fhall from time to time be neceffary to be employed in the affairs or bufinefs of the faid Corporation, and allow and pay reafonable falaries and allowances to the faid agents or fervants refpectively, and them, or any of them, from time to time remove or difplace, as they fhall fee caufe; and generally to act and do in all matters and things whatfoever, which they fhall judge neceffary, and may lawfully be done, for the well-order-

FIRST WARRANT.

and act according to the by-laws to be made and given unto them by the General Court; & where fuch by-laws are wanting, they, or major part of them, may direct and manage all the affairs of the Corporation;

and may appoint a Cafhier and Secretary, and all other officers;

and may allow them falaries, and difplace them, as they fee caufe.

F ing

FIRST
WARRANT.

No Governor, Deputy-Governor, nor Director, capable to be named, or chosen into the office of Cashier, or any other the offices of the Corporation.

ing and managing the said Corporation, and the affairs thereof, and do, enjoy, perform, and execute all the powers, authorities, privileges, acts, matters, and things, in relation to the said Corporation, as fully, to all intents and purposes, as if the same were done by the said Body Politic, hereby established, or by a General Court of the same, according to the true intent and meaning of these presents. Provided always, That the Governor, Deputy-Governor, nor any of the Directors of the said Company, either Ordinary or Extraordinary, shall be capable to be named or chosen into the office of Cashier, or any other the offices of the said Company. And, for the better carrying on the affairs of the said Company, and the more regular keeping just and exact accounts thereof, his Majesty doth, by these presents, will, direct, and appoint, that five at least of the Extraordinary Directors,

[43]

rectors, and four at least of the Ordinary Directors, shall and may, and they are hereby directed and required to meet together, at such time and times, as shall by the said Company in their General Courts, by their by-laws to be made pursuant to the powers hereby given, be directed, limited, and appointed, and inspect, state, and audite the accounts of the said Company; and the said accounts, when so stated, shall be signed and approved of by the said Extraordinary and Ordinary Directors. Provided always, That it shall and may be lawful to and for the said Company, in their General Courts, from time to time, by their by-laws to be by them made, pursuant to the powers to them hereby given, to alter, limit, and appoint the powers and authorities of the Extraordinary Directors; and that they shall not have or enjoy any other powers, except such as shall be given

to

FIRST WARRANT.

Five Extraordinary and four Ordinary Directors at least, to meet to state and audite the accounts, and sign and approve the same as often as directed by the by-laws.

The Extraordinary Directors to have no powers but such as shall be given to them, and allowed of by the General Courts.

FIRST WARRANT.

to them, and allowed of by the said General Courts, as aforesaid. And his Majesty doth hereby, for himself, his heirs, and successors, give full power to all and every the said Members, qualified as aforesaid, in their General Courts or Assemblies, by majority of their votes, as aforesaid, to make and constitute such by-laws and ordinances for and relating to the affairs and government of the said Corporation, and imposing mulcts and amerciaments upon offenders against the same, as to them shall seem meet, so that such by-laws be not contrary to the intent and meaning of these presents, or repugnant to the laws of his Majesty's realm, all which mulcts and amerciaments shall and may be received and recovered to the only use and behoof of the said Corporation and their successors, without any account, or other matter or thing to be therefore rendered to his Majesty, his heirs,

The General Courts to make and constitute by-laws, &c. and to impose mulcts and amerciaments upon offenders;

and

[45]

and fucceffors. And in cafe any per- *FIRST WARRANT.*
fon or perfons fhall refufe or neglect
to pay fuch mulcts and amerciaments,
fo impofed upon him, her, or them,
upon the time limited for that purpofe, it fhall and may be lawful to the
faid Court of Directors, and they are
hereby authorifed to retain the fame *which, if not duly*
out of all or any dividend or dividends *paid, may be re-*
tained out of their
that fhall become payable to fuch per- *dividends.*
fon or perfons fo refufing or neglect-
ing, as aforefaid. And his Majefty
doth hereby further, for himfelf, his
heirs, and fucceffors, give full power
to all and every the faid Members,
qualified as aforefaid, in their General
Courts or Affemblies, from time to time,
by majority of votes, as aforefaid, to
make fuch calls upon all and every the *The General*
Proprietors of the Capital Stock of the *Courts may make*
calls upon the Pro-
faid Corporation hereby erected, as to *prietors;*
the majority of fuch Members fo qualified as aforefaid, in their General
Courts, fhall feem proper, fo as fuch
calls

FIRST
WARRANT.

which are not in the whole to exceed 50l. upon the 100l. Capital, and no call to be above 10l. per cent. at a time.

Any perfon neglecting or refufing to pay fuch calls fhall not be allowed to tranffer or part with any part of their Stock.

calls fo to be made don't in the whole exceed fifty pounds upon every hundred pounds of the Subfcribed Capital of the faid Stock, and fo as not above ten pounds upon every hundred pounds of the faid Subfcribed Capital of the faid Stock be called at one time; and that fuch calls fo to be made, as aforefaid, fhall be paid in by the refpective Proprietors, within the time or times fo to be limited, by the order of fuch General Court for that purpofe, as aforefaid; and that no perfon or perfons who fhall refufe or neglect to pay in fuch calls, at the time or times for that purpofe limited, fhall be allowed to transfer or part with any fhare they refpectively have in the faid Stock, nor receive any dividends or profits on account thereof, till fuch calls fhall be by them refpectively paid. And that all and every perfon or perfons refufing or neglecting to pay the faid call or calls, fhall,

from

from and after the respective times such calls ought to have been paid, be charged and chargeable with interest for such calls, till the same are respectively paid; and that it shall and may be lawful to and for the said Governor, Deputy-Governor, and Court of Directors, or the majority of them so present, to detain all such dividends and profits, as such person or persons so neglecting or refusing to pay their calls would otherwise be entitled to, and apply the same for and towards payment of the said calls, which should have been respectively paid by them, with interest from such times as the same ought respectively to have been paid. Provided always, and for ascertaining and limiting in what manner, and under what rules the said Capital Stock shall and may be assignable and assigned, transferable and transferred, by such person or persons as shall, from time to time, have any interest

or

FIRST WARRANT.

Such calls chargeable with interest from the time they ought to be paid,

and their dividends may be detained, & applied for payment thereof.

FIRST
WARRANT.

Books for transfers to be kept at Edinburgh.

Form of transfers when made by the party himself.

or shares in the same, his Majesty doth hereby direct and appoint, That there shall be forthwith provided and constantly kept in the public office or offices of the said Corporation at Edinburgh, a book or books, wherein all assignments or transfers shall be entered. And his Majesty doth hereby, for himself, his heirs, and successors, by virtue of his prerogative royal, order, direct, limit, and appoint, that the method and manner of making all assignments and transfers of the said Capital Stock, or any part thereof, shall be by an entry in such book or books to be kept, as aforesaid, signed by the parties so assigning and transferring, in the words, or to the effect following, viz. *I A. B. this   day of   , in the year of our Lord   , do assign and transfer   , being all my interest or share, or (as the case may be) part of my interest or share in the Capital Stock or Fund of*

The

The Royal Bank of Scotland, *and all benefit arising thereby unto C. D. his executors, administrators, and assigns. Witness my hand, A. B.* Or, in case the party assigning be not personally present, then by an entry in the book or books, signed by some person thereunto lawfully authorised by letter of attorney or factory, under hand and seal, attested by two or more witnesses, in the words, or to the effect following, viz. *I A. B. this   day of   , in the year of our Lord   ; by virtue of a letter of attorney or authority, under the hand and seal of   ; dated the   day of   ; in the said year   , do, in the name and on the behalf of the said   , assign and transfer   , being all the interest or share (or as the case may be) part of the interest or share of the said   , in the Capital Stock or Fund of* The Royal Bank of Scotland, *and all benefits arising thereby un-*

FIRST WARRANT.

The form of transfers when made by an attorney.

G   *to*

[50]

FIRST WARRANT.

to   , his executors, administrators, and assignees. Witness my hand,

Form of acceptance of Stock.

Under which transfer the person or persons, bodies politic or corporate, to whom such assignment or transfer shall be made, or some other person by him or them lawfully authorised thereunto, shall sign his or their name or names, attesting, *That he or they do freely and voluntarily accept of the same;* and that the entry, signed as aforesaid, and no other way or method, shall be the manner and method used in the passing, assigning, and transferring the interest or shares in the said Capital Stock or Fund; and every such trans-

And no other method of transfer shall be valid.

fer and assignment shall be good and valid, and convey the estate and interest of the party assigning, of and in the Stock so assigned to the assignee thereof. And for the better prevent-

Letters of attorney to contain the names and designations of the writer and witnesses,

ing any fraud in making of transfers by letter of attorney, his Majesty doth hereby will and direct, That every

such

such letter of attorney or factory, so to be given, as aforesaid, shall contain the names and designations of the writers thereof, and the witnesses to the execution thereof, and the same shall be attested to have been duly executed by the persons giving such letter of attorney or factory, either by a notary public, or by a justice of the peace, or the minister of the parish, where the person giving such letter of attorney or factory resides. Provided always, That any person having any share or interest in the said Capital Stock or Fund, may dispose and devise the same by his or her last will and testament. But, however, that the executor or administrator shall not transfer the same, or be entitled to receive any dividend, until an extract of the testament be delivered to the Company, and until an entry or memorandum of so much of the said will as relates to the said Stock or Fund, be made in the book or books to be kept by,

-or

FIRST WARRANT.

and to be attested by a notary, justice of the peace, or minister of the parish, where the granter resides.

Any share of the Stock may be disposed of by last will & testament.

An extract of the testament is to be delivered to the Company, and a memorandum thereof entered in a book to be kept for that purpose.

[52]

FIRST WARRANT.

All the shares or interests in the Stock to be deemed personal estates,

and not to be liable to any arrestment or attachment.

A Court of Directors to consist of the Governor, Deputy-Governor, and Ordinary Directors, or any five of them at least,

wherein the Governor is to preside, and, in his absence, the Deputy-Governor.

or by order of the said Corporation for that purpose. Provided also, That the shares or interests of the several Proprietors in the said Company are and shall be deemed and taken to be personal or moveable estates, and, upon death, shall go to executors or administrators, and not be descendible to heirs; and the same shall not be liable to any arrestment or attachment that shall be laid thereupon, any law, usage, or custom to the contrary notwithstanding. Provided also, and his Majesty doth hereby, for himself, his heirs, and successors, will, direct, and appoint, That in every meeting of the said Governor, Deputy-Governor, and Court of Directors, the said Court to consist of the said Governor, Deputy-Governor, or five of the Ordinary Directors at least. And in case the said Governor or Deputy-Governor be present, such Governor, or, in his absence, such Deputy-Governor to preside;

fide; and, in cafe of the abfence of the Governor and Deputy-Governor, the major part of the Directors then prefent fhall and may chufe and appoint one of the faid Directors then prefent to be Prefident of that Court for the time being; and fhall, from time to time, in the abfence of the Governor and Deputy-Governor, appoint one of the faid Directors prefent, to prefide in every General Court of fuch Corporation; and, in default of fuch appointment, the General Court when met fhall and may appoint a Prefident of the fame General Court; which Prefident, when nominated by the Court of Directors, or General Court, for the time being refpectively, fhall, in all cafes of equality, have the cafting vote, but fhall have no vote, except in cafes of equality of votes. Provided alfo, That all matters and things, which the Governor, Deputy-Governor, and Directors of the faid Corporation

FIRST WARRANT.

In the abfence of both, any Director prefent may be chofen to prefide in that Court of Directors, or in any General Court of the Corporation;

and in default thereof, the General Court may chufe a Prefident;

The Prefident to have no vote, but in cafes of equality.

[54]

FIRST WARRANT.

Corporation shall, in manner aforesaid, order and direct to be done by Sub-Committees, or other persons appointed under them, shall and may, by virtue of such orders, be done by the said Sub-Committees, and other persons so appointed. And his Majesty doth likewise hereby, for himself, his heirs, and successors, will, appoint, and direct, That the Cashier of the Corporation hereby erected, or any other person by them lawfully authorised, shall and may, from time to time, receive from the said *Equivalent Company*, or any person by them lawfully authorised, the share and proportion of the said annual sum of Ten thousand pounds payable by virtue of the said act of parliament, as aforesaid, and dividends, in respect of such of the Stock of the said present *Equivalent Company*, so to be subscribed, as aforesaid; and that the same shall be paid to such person so empowered, without any fee or reward

The Court of Directors may name Committees to manage their affairs.

The Cashier of the Corporation, or any other person authorised by them to receive their proportion of the 10,000l. annuity,

which is to be paid without any fee or reward whatsoever.

[55]

ward whatsoever. And his Majesty doth hereby further, for himself, his heirs, and successors, will, direct, and appoint, That the said General Court of the said Corporation hereby erected, shall, and are hereby required, at two times in every year, to make and declare such dividend as they shall think proper to be paid, and payable to the respective Proprietors of the said Stock, at such two of the said quarterly Courts, hereby appointed and directed to be kept, as they shall think proper. Provided always, That no dividend shall be made to the Proprietors of the said Stock of the Company hereby erected, but out of the share and interest of the yearly annuity, or sum of Ten thousand pounds, payable to them as aforesaid, and out of the profits arising and to arise, by borrowing and lending of money, and dealing in the trade and business of Banking, as aforesaid. Provided always, That

FIRST WARRANT.

The GeneralCourt at two times in every year is to declare a dividend,

at such two of the quarterly Courts as they think fit.

No dividends to be made, but out of their share of the 10,000l. annuity, and the profits of banking.

[56]

FIRST WARRANT.

That it shall and may be lawful to and for the Company, hereby erected in their General Courts, from time to time, and as they shall think proper, and for the advantage of the said Corporation, and the Proprietors thereof, to repay all or any part of the said sum of fifty pounds per cent. that shall at any time have been called by them upon the Stock of the said Company. Provided always, That it shall and may be lawful to and for the Proprietors of the said Corporation hereby erected, or the majority of them, in any General Court of the said Company to be held as aforesaid, within the space of two years after the date hereof, to allow the Proprietors of all or any part of the Stock of the present *Equivalent Company*, who shall not have subscribed their said Stock on or before the twenty-ninth day of September one thousand seven hundred and twenty-seven years, being the

Calls upon the Stock may be repaid.

A General Court may assume such of the Proprietors of the Equivalent Stock, as shall not have subscribed before the 29th of September 1727, within two years from the date of the charter.

[57]

the term hereby limited for fubfcribing the fame, to fubfcribe all or fuch further and other part of the Stock of the faid Company into the Stock of the Corporation hereby erected, upon fuch terms and conditions, and at fuch times, as the majority of the Proprietors of the faid firft fubfcribed Stock in fuch General Courts, fhall limit, direct, and appoint. And his Majefty doth hereby declare and direct, That fuch Stock of the prefent *Equivalent Company,* fo to be fubfcribed in the terms aforefaid, fhall, from and after fuch fubfcription, be and be under the management, care, and direction of the Corporation hereby erected, from the time of fuch fubfcription, in the fame way and manner as the Stock to be fubfcribed on or before the faid twenty-ninth day of September one thoufand feven hundred and twenty-feven years, is hereby directed and appointed, and fhall and may, upon the

H terms

FIRST WARRANT.

Upon fuch terms and conditions, and at fuch times, as the majority of the firft fubfcribers fhall appoint in a General Court.

Such further fubfcriptions to be under the management of this Corporation, from the time of fubfcribing.

FIRST WARRANT.

terms and conditions fo to be limited and appointed, from the time of such fubfcription, as aforefaid, enjoy and have all the fame privileges and liberties as the Proprietors of the firft fubfcribed Stock fhall have and enjoy. And his Majefty doth, for himfelf, his heirs, and fucceffors, grant and declare, That thefe his letters patent fhall be in and by all things valid and effectual in the law, according to the true intent and meaning of the fame; and fhall be taken, conftrued, and adjudged in the moft favourable and beneficial fenfe, for the beft advantage of the faid Corporation, notwithftanding any mifrecital, defects, uncertainty, or imperfection in thefe his Majefty's letters patent. And his Majefty doth hereby, for himfelf, his heirs, and fucceffors, covenant, grant, and agree to and with the faid Corporation or Body Politic, and their fucceffors, That he, his heirs, and fucceffors, fhall and will,

And to enjoy the fame privileges, &c. with the firft fubfcribers.

The Charter to be conftrued in the moft favourable fenfe for the advantage of the Corporation.

from

from time to time, and at all times hereafter, upon the humble suit and request of the said Corporation or Body Politic, and their successors, give and grant unto them all such further and other privileges, authorities, matters, and things, for rendering more effectual this his grant, according to the true intent and meaning of these presents, which he or they can or may lawfully grant, and as shall be reasonably advised and devised by the counsel learned of the said Corporation or Body Politic for the time being, and shall be approved of by the Lord Advocate, or Solicitor General, in Scotland, of his Majesty, his heirs, or successors, on his or their behalf. And his Majesty doth further will and command, That this Charter do pass the said Great Seal *per saltum*, without passing any other seal or register. For doing whereof, this shall be, as well to the Director of our Chancery for writing

FIRST WARRANT.

His Majesty covenants to give such further privileges as he may lawfully grant;

which shall be devised by their own counsel, and approven of by the Lord Advocate or Solicitor General for Scotland, for the time.

FIRST
WARRANT.

ting the fame, as to the Keeper of the faid Seal, for caufing the faid Seal to be appended thereto, a fufficient warrant.—Given at our Court at St James's the thirty-firft day of May one thoufand feven hundred and twenty-feven, in the thirteenth year of our reign.

SECOND

SECOND

WARRANT

OF

THE CHARTER

CONFIRMING AND GRANTING

NEW PRIVILEGES

TO THE

Royal Bank of Scotland.

OUR *SOVEREIGN LORD* confidering,   Preamble, That, by an Act of Parliament made and paffed in the fifth year of his late Majefty's reign, entitled, *An Act for fettling certain yearly funds, payable out of the Revenues of* Scotland, *to fatisfy public Debts in* Scotland, *and other ufes mentioned in the Treaty of Union; and to difcharge the Equivalents claimed on behalf of* Scotland, *in the terms of the*
faid

[62]

SECOND WARRANT.

said Treaty; and for obviating all future disputes, charges, and expences con-

Reciting the act of Parliament 1719, concerning the L.10,000 Annuity payable to the Creditors of the Public in Scotland.

cerning these Equivalents; it is enacted, amongst other things, That yearly, and every year, from the Feast of the Nativity of St John the Baptist, one thousand seven hundred and nineteen years, the full sum of Ten thousand pounds of lawful money of Great Britain shall be a yearly Fund for the particular purposes in that act expressed concerning the same; and shall continue and be payable in the manner therein particularly expressed for ever, subject nevertheless to redemption by Parliament, according to a *proviso* in the said act contained in that behalf. And it is thereby further enacted, That it should and might be lawful to and for his Majesty, by letters patent un-

His Majesty authorised to incorporate the Proprietors of the debts stated to amount to L.248,550:0:9¼,

der the Great Seal of Great Britain, to incorporate all and every the Proprietors of the debts and sums of money, stated to amount to the principal sum

sum of Two hundred and thirty thousand three hundred and eight pounds nine shillings ten pence and five sixth parts of a penny, due to the creditors of the public in Scotland, on the twenty-fourth day of June one thousand seven hundred and fourteen years, and Eighteen thousand two hundred and forty-one pounds ten shillings ten pence and two thirds of a penny, stated due to William Paterson, Esq. making together Two hundred and forty-eight thousand five hundred and fifty pounds and nine pence halfpenny, to be one Body Politic and Corporate, by such name as his Majesty should think most proper, and that by such name the said Corporation should have perpetual succession, subject to such redemption, as in the said act is appointed: With such powers to do and perform all matters appertaining to them to do and perform, touching or concerning the said capital

SECOND WARRANT.

due to the creditors of the public in Scotland,

by such name as he should think fit.

SECOND
WARRANT.

tal fums, and the faid yearly fund payable in refpect thereof, as his Majefty by the fame letters patent fhould think fit to grant. And it was thereby enacted, That the faid capital fum, amounting to Two hundred forty-eight thoufand five hundred and fifty pounds and nine pence halfpenny, fhould be, and be deemed to be, the Capital or Joint Stock of the faid Corporation; and that the fhares of the Members of and in the fame fhould be from time to time affignable, tranfferable, and devifeable; in fuch manner as his Majefty by fuch letters patent fhould prefcribe and appoint, until the redemption thereof; and that the fame fhould be deemed to be perfonal or moveable eftates; and fhould go to executors or adminiftrators, and fhould not be liable to any arreftments or attachments that fhould be laid thereon. And it is thereby enacted, That all and every the Members of the

And the faid
L..248,550:0:9½,
fhould be the Capital or Joint Stock
of the Corporation,

and be deemed
perfonal or moveable eftates,

not liable to arreftments or attachments.

the said Corporation should have and be entitled to an annuity or yearly sum, in proportion to his or their share in the said capital sum and stock of Two hundred and forty-eight thousand five hundred and fifty pounds and nine pence halfpenny; and the said annuity should be paid in the manner in the said act mentioned, and to and for no other use, intent, or purpose whatsoever. And it was further enacted, That, above the said annuity of Ten thousand pounds per annum, there should be paid to the said Corporation and their successors, until the redemption of such annual sum, the further annual sum of Six hundred pounds per annum, towards the necessary charges of the management thereof, as in and by the said act of Parliament, amongst other clauses and things therein contained, relation being thereunto had, doth more fully and at large appear. And considering

SECOND WARRANT.

L. 600 per annum to be paid to the Corporation for charges of management.

SECOND
WARRANT.

ing, That his late Majesty King George the First, of glorious memory, by his letters patent, bearing date at Westminster, the twenty-first day of November, in the eleventh year of his reign, in pursuance of the said act of Parliament, and by virtue of his prerogative royal, and likewise of his especial grace, certain knowledge, and mere motion, did give, grant, make, ordain, declare, appoint, and establish, That all and every person or persons, natives and foreigners, bodies politic and corporate, who then were Proprietors of the debts and sums of money so stated to amount to Two hundred forty-eight thousand five hundred and fifty pounds and nine pence halfpenny, or who, by any lawful title, derived, or to be derived, from, by, or under the said Proprietors at any time thereafter, should have, and be entitled to any part, share, or interest therein, should be, and be called, one Body
Politic

Politic and Corporate of themselves, in deed and name, by the name of the EQUIVALENT COMPANY; and that such Corporation, and their successors, should have perpetual succession, subject to such redemption as is therein mentioned; and should and might have and use a common seal, and should, by that name, be capable to sue and be sued; and that the sum of Two hundred forty-eight thousand five hundred and fifty pounds and nine pence halfpenny, should be accepted, deemed, and esteemed the Capital or Joint Stock of the said Corporation, and all the Proprietors of such stock should be Members of the said Corporation; and that the said annuity of Ten thousand pounds per annum should be paid to the said Company or their Cashier, to be divided and distributed to and amongst the several Proprietors, in proportion to their respective shares in the said Capital or

Joint

SECOND WARRANT.

Recital of the charter creating the Proprietors of the foresaid debt into a Corporation, by the name of the EQUIVALENT COMPANY.

The foresaid L.248,550 : 0 : 9½ to be the Capital or Joint Stock of the EQUIVALENT COMPANY:

And the annuity of L.10,000, payable to the Company or their Cashier, to be divided amongst the Proprietors, according to their shares in the stock.

[68]

SECOND WARRANT.

The stock of the Company to be transferable.

The L.600 is payable to the EQUIVALENT COMPANY, or any person to be appointed by them, under their seal, to receive the same.

His Majesty covenants to give the EQUIVALENT COMPANY further powers and privileges upon their humble suit and request.

Joint Stock. And that his said Majesty did thereby further order and direct, limit, and appoint, That the said stock should be transferable and assignable; and all assignments and transfers of the said capital stock, or yearly fund, or any part thereof, should be in the manner, and according to the methods thereby directed: And likewise appointed, That the said annual sum of Six hundred pounds for charges of management, should be paid to the said Corporation, or such as they should authorise, under their common seal, to receive the same, for the uses of the said Corporation. And that his Majesty did thereby, for himself, his heirs, and successors, covenant, grant, and agree to and with the said Corporation and Body Politic, and their successors, That he, his heirs, and successors, should and would, from time to time, and at all times thereafter, upon the humble suit and request of the said

Corporation

Corporation or Body Politic; and their successors, give and grant unto them all such further and other powers, privileges, and authorities, matters and things, for rendering more effectual their said grant, according to the true intent and meaning of the said act, and of the said grant, which he or they could or might lawfully grant, subject to the power of redemption therein mentioned, as by the said grant or letters patent, passed under the Great Seal of Great Britain, relation being thereunto had, doth and may more fully at large appear. And whereas by charter or letters patent passed under the Seal appointed by the Treaty of Union to be kept in Scotland, in place of the Great Seal thereof, and bearing date the 31st day of May 1727, reciting to the effect before recited, and also reciting that the said Corporation of the *Equivalent Company*, by their most humble application to his said late Majesty, requested,

SECOND WARRANT.

Recital of the Charter granting the power of Banking, &c. in Scotland, upon petition of the EQUIVALENT COMPANY,

[70]

SECOND WARRANT.

To such of the Members as should subscribe their stock for that purpose.

Such subscribed stock only to be subject to the transactions of Banking, & thereafter to be transferable from the other stock of the EQUIVALENT COMPANY, and at Edinburgh only.

requested, That he would be graciously pleased, by letters patent under the Great Seal of Scotland, to enable such of the Proprietors of the said Corporation as should subscribe their stock for that purpose, to have the power of Banking in Scotland only, with liberty to borrow and lend upon security there; that the said Corporation might be for that purpose impowered to take subscriptions at Edinburgh from their Members, for such share of the stock as they shall incline to subject to such Trade or Banking, under such regulations as they by bye-laws should appoint; and that such subscribed stock only should be affected by the transactions relating to Banking, and (after being so subscribed) become transferable from the other stock of the Company, and at Edinburgh only; and would erect such subscribers into a Corporation for that purpose; and that such power of Banking, so established,

established, would manifestly tend to the great benefit and advantage of that part of the kingdom; his Majesty, being willing to give all proper encouragement to such an undertaking, therefore his said Majesty, in compliance with the said request, and by virtue of his prerogative royal, and of his especial grace, certain knowledge, and mere motion, and for the benefit of his subjects in that part of his united kingdoms, ordained a charter to be made and passed under the Seal appointed by the Treaty of Union to be kept in Scotland, in place of the Great Seal thereof, nominating, authorising, and appointing, as his Majesty thereby nominated, authorised, and appointed the persons therein named, or any three of them, in such way and manner as they, or the majority of them, should direct, to take and receive at Edinburgh all such voluntary subscriptions as should be made,

SECOND WARRANT.

A Charter ordained to pass the Seals of Scotland,

authorising the Directors of the said EQUIVALENT COMPANY, or any three of them, in such way as the majority of them shall direct,

to receive at Edinburgh all such voluntary subscrip-

[72]

SECOND WARRANT.

tions as should be made on or before the 29th day of September 1727, by the Proprietors of the said Company.

made, on or before the 29th day of September 1727 years, by any person or persons, Members or Proprietors of the said *Equivalent Company,* who had, or should have credit for stock in the books of the said Company at Edinburgh, at the time of such subscription, of all or any of such part or share of the stock of the said Equivalent Company, as he, she, or they, should think proper, for and towards raising a fund for the more effectually carrying on the said trade and business of Banking there, and the uses therein after mentioned; which said subscriptions the said Proprietors were thereby impowered to make, and the same should be fairly entered in books to be kept for that purpose, and the then present stock of the said Equivalent Company, so to be subscribed as aforesaid, should, from and after the time of such subscription, be under the order, management, and direction of

Which subscriptions are to be entered in books to be kept for that purpose.

The stock so subscribed, to be under the management of the Corporation hereby established.

of the Company thereby eſtabliſhed. And his Majeſty, by virtue of his ſaid prerogative, and likewiſe of his ſpecial grace, certain knowledge, and mere motion, gave, granted, made, ordained, conſtituted, declared, appointed, and eſtabliſhed, That all and every perſon or perſons, natives and foreigners, bodies politic and corporate, Proprietors of the ſaid ſtock, who ſhould ſubſcribe any ſhare or ſhares of the ſaid ſtock, and who, as executors, adminiſtrators, ſucceſſors, or aſſignees, or by any other lawful title, to be derived from, by, or under the ſaid ſubſcribers, at any time or times thereafter, ſhould have or be entitled to any part, ſhare, or intereſt of or in the ſaid ſtock ſo to be ſubſcribed as aforeſaid, ſhould be and be called one Body Politic and Corporate of themſelves, in deed and name, by the name of *The Royal Bank of Scotland*; and that ſuch Corporation, and their ſucceſſors, by

SECOND WARRANT.

The ſubſcribers to be called by the name of *The Royal Bank of Scotland*, and by that name to have perpetual ſucceſſion,

[74]

SECOND WARRANT.

and a common seal, be capable in law to sue and be sued, in any of the Courts within Scotland.

the said name, should have perpetual succession, and should and might have and use a common seal, and they and their successors, by the same name, should be able and capable in law, to sue and implead, pursue and defend, answer and be answered, in all or any of his Majesty's Courts within Scotland; and that they and their successors, by the name aforesaid, should and might be able and capable in law, to have, purchase, receive, possess, enjoy,

To purchase lands, &c. in Scotland, and to sell the same.

and retain to them and their successors, lands, rents, tenements, and hereditaments, of what kind, nature, or quality soever, in Scotland only; and also to sell, grant, demise, analzie, or dispone the same: And his Majesty did thereby, for himself, his heirs, and successors, grant unto the said Company of the *Royal Bank of Scotland*, and their successors for ever,

The Royal Bank to have the power of Banking within Scotland.

full power and liberty to exercise the rights and powers of Banking, in that part

part of the united kingdom called Scotland only; and in particular to lend to any person or persons, bodies politic or corporate, such sum and sums of money, as they should think fit, at any interest not exceeding lawful interest, on real or personal security; and particularly on pledges of any kind whatsoever, of any goods, wares, merchandises, or other effects whatsoever, in such way and manner as to the said Company should seem proper and convenient; and that the said Company might keep the money or cash of any person or persons, bodies politic and corporate whatsoever, and might borrow, owe, or take up in Scotland, on their bills or notes payable on demand, to be signed in such manner, and by such persons, as the Court of Directors therein after named should direct and appoint, or in such other manner as the said Court of Directors shall think fit, any sum or sums of money whatsoever;

SECOND WARRANT.

To lend any sum at any interest not exceeding lawful interest, upon personal and real security, and pledges of any kind.

The *Royal Bank* may keep the cash of other persons, and borrow, owe, and take up money on their bills or notes payable on demand.

SECOND WARRANT.

A prohibition to trade with the money or stock of the Company, in buying or selling wares of any sort.

Allowance nevertheless to deal in bills of exchange, in buying bullion, &c.

and selling wares *bona fide* pledged,

whatsoever. And his Majesty did thereby declare, direct, and appoint, That the said Company should not, at any time or times, deal or trade, or permit or suffer any person or persons whatsoever, either in trust or for the benefit of the same, to deal or trade with any of the stock, money, or effects, of or any ways belonging to the said Corporation, in the buying or selling of any goods, wares, or merchandises whatsoever; provided, that nothing therein contained should any ways be construed to extend to hinder the said Corporation from dealing in bills of exchange, or in buying or selling bullion, gold, or silver in Scotland only, or extend to hinder the said Corporation from selling any goods, wares, merchandises, or effects whatsoever, which should really and *bona fide* be pledged, left, or deposited with the said Corporation, for money lent and advanced thereon, and which should not

be

be redeemed at the time agreed on, or from felling such lands, rents, tenements, or hereditaments, as they should purchase, in virtue of the power thereby given, or from selling such goods as should or might be the produce of lands purchased by the said Corporation. And for the better accomplishment of the ends and intentions proposed by the erecting of the said Corporation, and for making and establishing a continual succession of fit persons to be Managers and Directors of the said Corporation, it was thereby ordained and appointed, That there should be, from time to time, a Governor, Deputy-Governor, nine Ordinary Directors, and nine Extraordinary Directors, to be chosen out of the Members of the said Company; who were to have such qualifications, and to be chosen annually, in the manner and according to the rules and directions therein mentioned; and that five

SECOND WARRANT.
and lands, &c. purchased, and the produce thereof.

That there shall be, from time to time, a Governor, Deputy-Governor, nine Ordinary, & nine Extraordinary Directors, for managing the affairs of the Corporation. The Governor, Deputy-Governor, and nine Ordinary Directors, or any five of them, to be called *A Court of Directors*.

SECOND WARRANT.

five or more should be called *A Court of Directors*, for ordering, managing, and directing all affairs of the said Corporation, in manner therein mention-

No Governor, Deputy-Governor, or Director, nor any officer or servant under them, shall be capable to act, until they have taken the oaths to the Government.

ed; and no Governor, Deputy-Governor, or Director, or any officer nominated by them, should be capable to sit, vote, or act, or to exercise, use, or discharge any such office, until he had first taken and subscribed the several oaths which then were, or by any subsequent law, should be directed to be taken by all persons bearing or holding any office, civil or military, under his Majesty, his heirs, and successors. And it is thereby further di-

The Court of Directors, may call General Courts of Proprietors, as prescribed;

rected, That the said Governor, Deputy-Governor, and Court of Directors, should have power and liberty, from time to time, to call General Courts of all the Proprietors, upon giving such notice as therein is prescribed, and there to dispatch any business relating to the government or affairs

fairs of the Corporation, and to remove or difplace the faid Governor, Deputy-Governor, and any of the Directors, for any mifdemeanours or abufe of their office, and elect and chufe new ones in their room, in manner therein mentioned; and to make bye-laws, conftitutions, orders, rules, for managing the bufinefs of the faid Corporation: And that fuch Court of Directors might appoint a Secretary and all other officers, and difplace them as they fhould fee caufe. And, for the better carrying on the affairs of the faid Corporation, the faid Court of Directors, or any nine of them, were directed to infpect, ftate, and audite the accounts of the Company; and fign and approve thereof, in manner therein directed; and power was thereby given to the General Courts of the faid Company, from time to time, by majority of votes, to make fuch calls upon all and every the Proprietors of the faid

SECOND WARRANT.

and remove or difplace the Governor, Deputy-Governor, & any of the Directors, for mifdemeanours, & chufe new ones;

and appoint a Secretary, and other officers, and difplace them as they fee caufe;

and infpect, ftate, and audite the accounts of the Company;

The General Courts may make calls upon the Proprietors;

SECOND
WARRANT.

which are not to exceed 50l. upon the 100l. Capital, and no call to be above 10l. per cent. at a time.

Any person neglecting to pay such calls shall not be allowed to transfer their Stock, nor receive any dividends or profits till such calls be paid.

said Stock and Corporation, as to the majority of such General Court should seem proper, so as such calls so to be made do not in the whole exceed fifty pounds upon every hundred pounds of the Subscribed Capital of the said Stock, and so as not above ten pounds in the hundred pounds of the said Subscribed Capital of the said Stock be called at one time; and that such calls should be paid in by the Proprietors, within the time or times so limited by such General Court; and that no person who should refuse or neglect to pay in such calls, should be allowed to transfer or part with any share they respectively had in the said Stock, nor receive any dividends or profits on account thereof, till such calls should by them respectively be paid. And for ascertaining and limiting in what manner, and under what rules the said Capital Stock should and might be assigned and transferred, it was thereby further directed,

directed, That there should be forthwith provided and constantly kept in the public office of the said Corporation at Edinburgh, a book or books, wherein all assignments or transfers should be entered, and the said stock should be transferable and transferred, according to the methods and forms therein particularly prescribed and set down; and that any person having any share or interest in the said Stock might dispose and devise the same by his or her last will and testament; and that all such shares or interests in such Stock should be deemed personal estates, and not be liable to any arrestment or attachment. And it was further declared, That the Cashier of the said Corporation, or any other person by them lawfully authorised, should, from time to time, receive from the said *Equivalent Company*, or any person by them lawfully authorised, their share and proportion of the said annual

SECOND WARRANT.

Books for transfers to be kept at Edinburgh.

Any share of the Stock may be disposed of by last will & testament.

The Stock not liable to any arrestment or attachment.

The Cashier of the Corporation, or any other person authorised to receive their proportion of the 10,000 l. annuity.

[82]

SECOND WARRANT.

annual sum of Ten thousand pounds payable by virtue of the said recited act of parliament and dividends, in respect of such of the said Stock of the said *Equivalent Company*, so to be subscribed; and that the General Court of the said Company should, at two terms in the year, declare such dividends as they should think proper to be paid to the respective Proprietors. Provided no dividend should be made but out of the share and interest of the yearly annuity of Ten thousand pounds, and out of the profit arising by borrowing and lending of money, and dealing in the trade and business of Banking; and that such General Court, from time to time, as they should see proper, might repay all or any part of the said sum of fifty pounds per cent. that should at any time have been called by them upon the Stock of the said Company. And his Majesty did thereby, for himself, his heirs, and successors,

The General Court, at two times in every year, is to declare a dividend.

No dividend to be made, but out of their share of the 10,000l. annuity, and the profits of Banking.

Calls upon the Stock may be repaid.

fors, covenant, grant, and agree to and with the said Corporation and their successors, that he, his heirs, and successors, should and would, from time to time, and at all times thereafter, upon the humble suit and request of the said Corporation and their successors, give and grant unto them all such further and other privileges, authorities, matters, and things, for rendering more effectual the said grant, according to the true intent and meaning thereof, which he or they could or might lawfully grant, and as should be reasonably advised and devised by the counsel learned of the said Corporation for the time being, and should be approved by the Lord Advocate or Solicitor General in Scotland, of his Majesty, his heirs, and successors, on his or their behalf, as by the said grant or letters patent, passed under the Seal appointed by the Treaty of Union to be kept in Scotland, in place of the

SECOND WARRANT.

His Majesty to give such further privileges as he may lawfully grant;

which shall be devised by their own counsel, and approven of by the Lord Advocate or Solicitor General for Scotland.

the

[84]

SECOND
WARRANT.

Recital of the petition of The Royal Bank to his Majesty.

That in purfuance of the said letters patent, Proprietors of the Equivalent Company did subscribe Stock for the purposes in the said charter to the extent of 111,000l.

That the annuity payable to the Proprietors of Equivalent, & shares subscribed into The Royal Bank, being subject to redemption, a doubt might arise, Whether, upon such redemption, The Royal Bank might cease;

the Great Seal thereof, relation being thereunto had, doth and may more fully and at large appear. And confidering that the said Corporation have, by their moſt humble application to his Majeſty, repreſenting, That, in purſuance of the ſaid letters patent, certain of the Proprietors of the ſaid *Equivalent Company* did ſubſcribe parts and ſhares of the ſaid Stock, for the purpoſes in the ſaid charter or letters patent mentioned, to the extent of One hundred and eleven thouſand pounds; and that they had for ſome years carried on the buſineſs of Banking, to the great benefit and advantage of that part of the united kingdom in general, and in particular to merchants carrying on and advancing trade: And further repreſenting, That the annuity to which the Proprietors of the *Equivalent Company*, and in conſequence the ſhares ſubſcribed into *The Royal Bank of Scotland*, being ſubject

to

to redemption, a doubt might arise, {SECOND WARRANT.} Whether, upon the redemption of the capital sum of the said *Equivalent Company* by Parliament, *The Royal Bank of Scotland* might cease and determine; and that it might also be doubted,— Whether, in the case of redemption, the said sum of One hundred and eleven thousand pounds must not be divided amongst the Proprietors, according to their respective interests in the said Stock at the time of redemption: And further representing, That it was found by experience that the present Capital of the said Bank was not sufficient to answer the several good ends and purposes of their erection; and that the Proprietors humbly apprehended, that the addition of any sum not exceeding Forty thousand pounds to the present Capital, making in the whole the sum of One hundred and fifty-one thousand pounds, might facilitate their operations, and enable them

{marginalia: and, whether the said sum of 111,000l. must not be divided amongst the Proprietors.}

{marginalia: That the present Capital of the said Bank was not sufficient to answer the purposes of their erection;}

{marginalia: the addition of a sum not exceeding 40,000l. to the present Capital, making in the whole 151,000l. might facilitate their operations.}

SECOND
WARRANT.

them to be further useful in that part of the united kingdom, Whether that addition should be made by subscribing a further sum of Equivalent Stock, heritable land security, or any other way that should appear safe to the said Corporation; and therefore praying,

That his Majesty would ratify and confirm their privileges, & remove all doubts concerning their subsisting, in case of redemption, and to enlarge their Capital to any sum not exceeding 40,000l. by subscriptions of Equivalent Stock, land security, or any other way.

that we would be graciously pleased, by letters patent under the Great Seal of Scotland, to ratify and confirm their privileges, authorities, and rights formerly granted, and to remove all doubts concerning the subsisting of the said Corporation, in case of redemption by Parliament; and to authorise and impower the Proprietors of the Royal Bank to enlarge their Capital to any sum not exceeding Forty thousand pounds, by taking in subscriptions of Equivalent Stock by heritable land security, or by any other way that the Directors of *The Royal Bank*, with consent of their General Court of Proprietors, shall judge safe and

and beneficial to the Bank: Alfo, that the Proprietors of the faid fum of One hundred and eleven thoufand pounds Equivalent Stock, may be impowered, by authority of a General Court of Proprietors, to take, acquit, and difcharge the Public of the aforefaid fum, and to lay out the fame in fuch way and on fuch fecurity as the Directors aforefaid fhall judge fafe; to the end that a fure and permanent fund may ftill fubfift for the credit of the Bank, and the fafety of fuch as deal with them. And confidering, fuch petition has been referred to the Lord Advocate in Scotland for his opinion, what might be reafonable and fitting for his Majefty to do therein; and his Majefty having taken into his confideration the faid petition, and the report thereupon made by the Lord Advocate for Scotland, and being willing to give all proper encouragement to fuch an undertaking, therefore his Majefty,

SECOND WARRANT.

The Proprietors, by authority of a General Court, to take & difcharge the Public of the aforefaid 111,000l. and lay out the fame as the Directors fhall judge fafe.

The above petition, and a report thereupon, having been confidered,

SECOND WARRANT.

a charter ordained to pass the Seals of Scotland,

confirming all privileges granted to The Royal Bank.

sty, in compliance with the said request, and by virtue of his prerogative royal, and of his especial grace, certain knowledge, and mere motion, and for the benefit of his subjects in that part of the united kingdom, ordains a charter to be made and passed under the Seal appointed by the Treaty of Union to be kept in Scotland, in place of the Great Seal thereof, ratifying and confirming, as we do hereby ratify and confirm, all the privileges, authorities, and rights, formerly granted to the said Company or Corporation of *The Royal Bank of Scotland*, by the said charter or letters patent, bearing date the thirty-first day of May one thousand seven hundred and twenty-seven, as aforesaid, in as ample manner and form, as if the same were all herein particularly mentioned and repeated. And to the end that the said *Royal Bank of Scotland* may be the better encouraged to proceed in so laudable

SECOND WARRANT.

laudable an undertaking of Banking, and so much for the benefit of the subjects of that part of the united kingdom; and considering, That the present Capital of the said Company of *The Royal Bank of Scotland*, is not sufficient to answer the several good ends and purposes of their erection, and that the addition of a sum to their present Capital may facilitate their operations, and enable them to be further useful to that part of the united kingdom, his Majesty hereby gives full power and authority to the Governor, Deputy-Governor, and Directors of the said Company of *The Royal Bank of Scotland*, by and with the direction and approbation of a General Court of the Proprietors thereof, to enlarge their present Capital to any sum not exceeding Forty thousand pounds, and that either by taking subscriptions of other Equivalent Stock not already subscribed into the said Bank, or by taking

And authorising the Governor, Deputy-Governor, & Directors of the said Company, with approbation of a General Court of Proprietors, to enlarge their present capital to any sum not exceeding 40,000*l*.

SECOND
WARRANT.

The Directors to receive subscriptions in such way as the General Court of Proprietors shall direct,

for completing the additional stock of 40,000l.

taking in subscriptions of certain sums of money upon land security, or any other ways and means that the said Directors of *The Royal Bank of Scotland*, by the consent of the said General Court of the Proprietors, shall judge most safe and beneficial to the Corporation of the said *Royal Bank*; and to that end, his Majesty does by these presents authorise and impower the said Directors to take and receive such subscriptions, in such way and manner as the General Court of the said Proprietors shall direct: And for completing the said additional Stock of Forty thousand pounds, it shall and may be lawful to and for the Proprietors of the said Company of *The Royal Bank*, or the majority of them, in any General Court of the said Company, to be held as in the said former charter is mentioned and directed, either to allow the Proprietors of such part of the Equivalent Stock, to subscribe

scribe such further or other part of the Stock of the said Company into the Stock of the said Company of *The Royal Bank*, not exceeding in the whole the Sum of Forty thousand pounds, upon such terms and conditions, and at such times as the majority of the Proprietors of *The Royal Bank of Scotland*, in such General Courts, shall limit and appoint; or it shall and may be lawful for the majority of the Proprietors of the said *Royal Bank of Scotland*, to take in such additional Stock of Forty thousand pounds by a voluntary subscription, either of money upon heritable security, or otherways, and upon such terms and conditions, and at such times as the majority of the Proprietors of the said Company of *The Royal Bank of Scotland*, in such General Court, shall limit, direct, and appoint. And his Majesty doth hereby declare and direct, That such Stock of the

Equivalent

SECOND WARRANT.

To allow the Proprietors of Equivalent Stock to subscribe such part of the Stock of the said Company into the Stock of *The Royal Bank*, not exceeding 40,000 l.;

or to take such additional stock by a voluntary subscription, either of money, heritable security, or otherwise.

Equivalent Company, fo to be fubfcribed in the terms aforefaid, and fuch fubfcriptions fo to be made in money upon heritable fecurity, or otherways, fhall, from and after fuch fubfcription, be and be under the management, care, and direction of the Corporation or Company of *The Royal Bank* from the time of fuch fubfcription, in the fame way and manner as the Stock formerly fubfcribed was, by the faid former charter or letters patent, directed and appointed; and fhall and may, upon the terms and conditions fo to be limited and appointed, from the time of fuch fubfcription, as aforefaid, have all the fame privileges and liberties as the Proprietors of the firft fubfcribed Stock fhall have and enjoy; and that fuch new Stock, fo to be fubfcribed, fhall be transferable in the fame way and manner, and upon the fame terms and conditions as the prefent Stock of the faid Company is now transferable,

Second Warrant.
The ftock fo fubfcribed, &c. to be under the direction of the Corporation of *The Royal Bank*, as the ftock formerly fubfcribed.

To have the fame privileges as the Proprietors of the the firft fubfcribed ftock.

Transferable in the fame way as the prefent ftock.

transferable, by virtue of or under the said charter of the thirty-first day of May, in the year one thousand seven hundred and twenty-seven; and the Proprietors of such subscribed Stock shall be entitled to have and receive the same, or the like dividends, as shall from time to time be declared upon the present Capital of the said Corporation or Company. And his Majesty, for the better encouragement of the said *Royal Bank* to proceed in and continue their undertaking of Banking so much for the benefit of the subjects of that part of our united kingdom, declares and directs, That in case the Parliament of Great Britain shall, at any time or times, think proper to redeem the said Equivalent Stock, or such part thereof as has been or shall be subscribed into the said Company of *The Royal Bank of Scotland*, that the said Corporation or Company of *The Royal Bank of Scotland*, notwithstanding

SECOND WARRANT.

For the better encouragement of *The Royal Bank*, in case the Parliament shall redeem the Equivalent Stock, or such part as has or shall be subscribed into *The Royal Bank*, that the Corporation, notwithstanding thereof, shall continue and have perpetual succession, and enjoy all privileges formerly granted,

standing thereof, shall and may, after such redemption as aforesaid, continue for ever, and have perpetual succession, and enjoy all the privileges, benefits, and advantages whatsoever, given and granted to them by the said recited charter or letters patent, except the share or interest in the said annual fund of Ten thousand pounds as aforesaid, as if no such redemption were had or made; and from and after such redemption, all persons having any share or interest, or stock paid into or gained by the said Company, to carry on the trade of the said Company, shall be and be deemed Members of the said Company, and be entitled to all the benefits and privileges and advantages thereof, in proportion to their respective shares and interest in the said money or stock as aforesaid; and the said money or stock so paid, or to be paid, shall be assignable or transferable in such and the like manner,

mutatis

SECOND WARRANT.

except the share in the annual fund of 10,000l.

After redemption, all persons having interest or stock paid into or gained by the said Company, to carry on the trade of the Company, shall be deemed Members, and entitled to all advantages thereof;

and the stock so paid, or to be paid, shall be transferable, in like manner as the shares in

mutatis mutandis, as the shares in the Capital Stock and yearly Fund are now assignable or may be assigned; and that, upon such redemption as aforesaid, the Proprietors of the said Stock in the said *Royal Bank*, or the majority of them in a General Court, shall and may, and they are hereby impowered and authorised to give sufficient authority to their Court of Directors, or such other person or persons as they shall please to nominate and appoint, to receive the money that shall be paid or payable to the Company or Corporation, upon such redemption as aforesaid, and give receipts, acquittances, or discharges for the same; and also, That it shall and may be lawful to and for the majority of the said Proprietors of the said Company and Corporation present at their General Court or Courts, and they are hereby impowered, and authorised to impower their said Court

the Capital Stock and yearly fund are now assignable.

The Proprietors in a General Court, or majority of them, impowered to give sufficient authority to their Court of Directors, or such persons as they shall nominate, to receive the money payable to the Company upon such redemption as aforesaid, and discharge the same;

SECOND WARRANT.

of Directors, from time to time, to lay out and invest the money that shall, upon such redemption, be paid as aforesaid, upon such security and securities as the said majority of the Proprietors in such General Court shall think fit to direct and appoint; and that the interest and produce arising by and from such money, or the securities taken for the same, shall be divided to and amongst the Proprietors of the Stock of *The Royal Bank*, in such way and manner, and by such methods, as the General Court of the said Company or Corporation, or the majority of them, shall direct and determine; and that the said money so paid in, and the securities taken for the same, shall be under the direction of the General Courts of the Corporation, and the Governor, Deputy-Governor, and Directors of the said Company or Corporation, in the same way and manner, and subject to the same

and to impower the Court of Directors, from time to time, to lay out the money that shall upon redemption be paid, upon such security as the majority of the Proprietors in such General Court shall think fit to appoint.

The interest arising from such money, or securities for the same, to be divided amongst the Proprietors, in such way as the General Court of the said Company, or majority of them, shall direct; and the money so paid, & securities taken for the same, shall be under the direction of the General Courts of the Corporation, and Governor, Deputy-Governor, and Directors, in the same way as the present Capital Stock.

same directions and authorities as the present Capital Stock of the said Corporation or Company are now under; to the end, that a sure and permanent fund may subsist for the credit of the said Bank, and security of such as deal with them. Provided always, That no dividend shall be made to the Proprietors of the said Stock of the said Company after such redemption as aforesaid, but out of the interest of money payable to them upon such redemption as aforesaid, and out of the profit arising and to arise by borrowing and lending of money, and dealing in the trade and business of Banking, as aforesaid. And his Majesty doth, for himself, his heirs, and successors, grant and declare, That these his letters patent shall be in and by all things valid and effectual in the law, according to the true intent and meaning of the same, and shall be taken, and construed, and adjudged, in the most

SECOND WARRANT.

That a sure fund may subsist for the credit of the Bank, and security of such as deal with them.

No dividend to be made, but out of the interest of money payable upon redemption, and the profits of Banking.

The Charter to be construed in the most favourable sense for the advantage of the Corporation.

SECOND WARRANT.

His Majesty covenants to give such further privileges as he may lawfully grant;

which shall be devised by their own counsel, and approven of by the Lord Advocate or Solicitor General for Scotland, for the time.

moſt favourable and beneficial ſenſe, for the beſt advantage of the ſaid Corporation, notwithſtanding any miſreсital, defaults, uncertainty, or imperfection, in theſe his Majeſty's letters patent. And his Majeſty doth hereby, for himſelf, his heirs, and ſucceſſors, covenant, grant, and agree to and with the ſaid Corporation or Body Politic, and their ſucceſſors, That he, his heirs, and ſucceſſors, ſhall and will, from time to time, and at all times hereafter, upon the humble ſuit and requeſt of the ſaid Corporation or Body Politic, and their ſucceſſors, give and grant unto them all ſuch further and other privileges, authorities, matters, and things, for rendering more effectual this his grant, according to the true intent and meaning of theſe preſents, which he or they can or may lawfully grant, and as ſhall be reaſonably adviſed and deviſed by the counſel learned of the ſaid Corporation or Body

Body Politic for the time being, and shall be approved of by the Lord Advocate or Solicitor General in Scotland, of his Majesty, his heirs, and successors, on his or their behalf. And his Majesty doth further will and command, That this Charter do pass the Great Seal *per saltum*, without passing any other seal or register. For doing whereof, this shall be, as well to the Director of our Chancery for writing the same, as to the Keeper of the said Seal, for causing the said Seal to be appended thereto, a sufficient warrant.—Given at our Court at St James's this first day of November one thousand seven hundred and thirty-eight, in the twelfth year of our reign.

THIRD

WARRANT

OF

THE CHARTER

CONFIRMING AND GRANTING

NEW PRIVILEGES

TO THE

Royal Bank of Scotland.

Preamble.   OUR *SOVEREIGN LORD* confidering, That, by an Act of Parliament made and paffed in the 5th year of the reign of his Majefty King George Firft, entitled, *An Act for fettling certain yearly funds, payable out of the Revenues of* Scotland, *to fatisfy public Debts in* Scotland, *and other ufes mentioned in the Treaty of Union; and to difcharge the Equivalents claimed on behalf of* Scotland,

Scotland, *in the terms of the said Treaty; and for obviating all future disputes, charges, and expences concerning these Equivalents;* it is enacted, amongst other things, That yearly, and every year, from the Feast of the Nativity of St John the Baptist, in the year one thousand seven hundred and nineteen, the full sum of Ten thousand pounds of lawful money of Great Britain shall be a yearly Fund for the particular purposes in that act expressed, and shall continue and be payable for ever, in the manner therein directed, subject nevertheless to redemption by Parliament, according to a *proviso* in the said act. And it is thereby further enacted, That it should and might be lawful to and for his Majesty, by letters patent under the Great Seal of Great Britain, to incorporate all and every the Proprietors of the debts and sums of money, stated to amount to the principal sum of Two hundred and thirty thousand

THIRD WARRANT.

Reciting the act of Parliament 1719, concerning the L.10,000 Annuity payable to the Creditors of the Public in Scotland.

His Majesty authorised to incorporate the Proprietors of the debts stated to amount to L..248,550 : 0 : 9¼.

[102]

THIRD WARRANT.

due to the creditors of the public in Scotland,

thousand three hundred and eight pounds nine shillings ten pence and five sixth parts of a penny, due to the creditors of the public in Scotland, on the twenty-fourth day of June in the year one thousand seven hundred and fourteen, and Eighteen thousand two hundred and forty-one pounds ten shillings ten pence and two thirds of a penny, stated due to William Paterson, Esq. making together Two hundred and forty-eight thousand five hundred and fifty pounds and nine pence halfpenny, to be one Body Politic and Corporate, by such name as his Majesty

by such name as he should think fit.

should think most proper, and that by such name the said Corporation should have perpetual succession, subject to such redemption as in the said act is appointed; with such powers to do and perform all matters appertaining to them to do and perform, touching or concerning the said capital sums, and the said yearly fund payable

able in respect thereof, as his Majesty by the same letters patent should think fit to grant. And it was thereby enacted, That the said capital sum, amounting to Two hundred and forty-eight thousand five hundred and fifty pounds and nine pence halfpenny, should be, and be deemed to be, the Capital or Joint Stock of the said Corporation; and that the shares of the Members of and in the same should be from time to time assignable, transferable, and deviseable, in such manner as his Majesty by such letters patent should prescribe and appoint, until the redemption thereof; and that the same should be deemed to be personal or moveable estates, and should go to executors or administrators, and should not be liable to any arrestments or attachments that should be laid thereon. And it is thereby enacted, That all and every the Members of the said Corporation should have and be

THIRD WARRANT.

And the said L.248,550 : 0 : 9½, should be the Capital or Joint Stock of the Corporation,

and be deemed personal or moveable estates,

not liable to arrestments or attachments.

THIRD
WARRANT.

be entitled to an annuity or yearly sum, in proportion to his or their share in the said capital sum and stock of Two hundred and forty-eight thousand five hundred and fifty pounds and nine pence halfpenny; and the said annuity should be paid in the manner in the said act mentioned, and to and for no other use, intent, or purpose whatsoever. And it was further enacted, That, above the said annuity of Ten thousand pounds per annum, there should be paid to the said Corporation and their successors, until the redemption of such annual sum,

L. 600 per annum to be paid to the Corporation for charges of management.

the further annual sum of Six hundred pounds per annum, towards the necessary charges of the management thereof, as in and by the said act of Parliament, amongst other clauses and things therein contained, relation being thereunto had, doth more fully and at large appear. And considering, That his said Majesty King George

the

the First, of glorious memory, by his letters patent, bearing date at Westminster, the twenty-first day of November, in the eleventh year of his reign, in pursuance of the said act of Parliament, and by virtue of his prerogative royal, and likewife of his especial grace, certain knowledge, and mere motion, did give, grant, make, ordain, declare, appoint, and establish, That all and every person or persons, natives and foreigners, bodies politic and corporate, who then were Proprietors of the debts and sums of money so stated to amount to Two hundred forty-eight thousand five hundred and fifty pounds and nine pence halfpenny, or who, by any lawful title, derived, or to be derived, from, by, or under the said Proprietors at any time thereafter, should have, and be entitled to any part, share, or interest therein, should be, and be called, one Body Politic and Corporate of themselves,

THIRD WARRANT.

Recital of the charter erecting the Proprietors of the foresaid debt into a Corporation, by the name of the EQUIVALENT COMPANY.

in

THIRD
WARRANT.

in deed and name, by the name of the EQUIVALENT COMPANY; and that fuch Corporation, and their fucceffors, fhould have perpetual fucceffion, fubject to fuch redemption as is therein mentioned, and fhould and might have and ufe a common feal, and fhould, by that name, be capable to fue and be fued; and that the fum of Two hundred forty-eight thoufand five hundred and fifty pounds and nine pence halfpenny, fhould be accepted, deemed, and efteemed the Capital or Joint Stock of the faid Corporation, and all the Proprietors of fuch ftock fhould be Members of the faid Corporation; and that the faid annuity of Ten thoufand pounds per annum fhould be paid to the faid Company or their Cafhier, to be divided and diftributed to and amongft the feveral Proprietors, in proportion to their refpective fhares in the faid Capital or Joint Stock. And his faid Majefty did

The forefaid L.248,550 : 0 : 9¼ to be the Capital or Joint Stock of the EQUIVALENT COMPANY:

And the annuity of L.10,000, payable to the Company or their Cafhier, to be divided amongft the Proprietors, according to their fhares in the ftock.

[107]

did thereby further order and direct, limit, and appoint, That the said stock should be transferable and assignable; and all assignments and transfers of the said capital stock, or yearly fund, or any part thereof, should be in the manner, and according to the methods thereby directed: And likewise appointed, That the said annual sum of Six hundred pounds for charges of management, should be paid to the said Corporation, or such as they should authorise, under their common seal, to receive the same, for the uses of the said Corporation, as by the said grant or letters patent, passed under the Great Seal of Great Britain, relation being thereunto had, doth and may more fully and at large appear. And whereas by charter or letters patent, passed under the Seal appointed by the Treaty of Union to be kept in Scotland, in place of the Great Seal thereof, and bearing date the 31st of May

THIRD WARRANT.

The stock of the Company to be transferable.

The L.600 is payable to the Equivalent Company, or any person to be appointed by them, under their seal, to receive the same.

Recital of the Charter granting the power of Banking, &c. in Scotland, upon petition of the Equivalent Company,

THIRD
WARRANT.

May in the year one thousand seven hundred and twenty-seven, reciting to the effect before recited, and also reciting that the said Corporation of the *Equivalent Company*, by their most humble application to his said Majesty, requested, That he would be graciously pleased, by letters patent under the Great Seal of Scotland, to enable such

to such of the Members as should subscribe their stock for that purpose.

of the Proprietors of the said Corporation as should subscribe their stock for that purpose, to have the power of Banking in Scotland only, with liberty to borrow and lend upon security there; that the said Corporation might be for that purpose impowered to take subscriptions at Edinburgh from their Members, for such share of the stock as they shall incline to subject to such Trade or Banking, under such regulations as they by bye-laws

Such subscribed stock only to be subject to the transactions of Banking, & thereafter to be trans-

should appoint; and that such subscribed stock only should be affected by the transactions relating to Banking, and

and (after being so subscribed) become transferable from the other stock of the Company, and at Edinburgh only; and would erect such subscribers into a Corporation for that purpose; and that such power of Banking, so established, would manifestly tend to the great benefit and advantage of that part of the kingdom; his Majesty, being willing to give all proper encouragement to such an undertaking, therefore his said Majesty, in compliance with the said request, and by virtue of his prerogative royal, and of his especial grace, certain knowledge, and mere motion, and for the benefit of his subjects in that part of his united kingdom, ordained a charter to be made and passed under the Seal appointed by the Treaty of Union to be kept in Scotland, in place of the Great Seal thereof, nominating, authorising, and appointing, as his Majesty thereby nominated, authorised,

THIRD WARRANT.

ferable from the other stock of the EQUIVALENT COMPANY, *and at Edinburgh only.*

A Charter ordained to pass the Seals of Scotland,

THIRD WARRANT.

authorising the Directors of the said Equivalent Company, or any three of them, in such way as the majority of them shall direct, to receive at Edinburgh all such voluntary subscriptions as should be made on or before the 29th day of September 1727, by the Proprietors of the said Company.

sed, and appointed the persons therein named, or any three of them, in such way and manner as they, or the majority of them, should direct, to take and receive at Edinburgh all such voluntary subscriptions as should be made, on or before the 29th day of September in the year 1727, by any person or persons, Members or Proprietors of the said *Equivalent Company*, who had, or should have credit for stock in the books of the said Company at Edinburgh, at the time of such subscription, of all or any of such part or share of the stock of the said Equivalent Company, as he, she, or they, should think proper, for and towards raising a fund for the more effectually carrying on the said trade and business of Banking there, and the uses therein after mentioned; which said subscrip-

Which subscriptions are to be entered in books to be kept for that purpose.

tions the said Proprietors were thereby impowered to make, and the same should be fairly entered in books to be kept

kept for that purpose; and the then present stock of the said Equivalent Company, so to be subscribed as aforesaid, should, from and after the time of such subscription, be under the order, management, and direction of the Company thereby established. And his Majesty, by virtue of his said prerogative, and likewise of his special grace, certain knowledge, and mere motion, gave, granted, made, ordained, constituted, declared, appointed, and established, That all and every person or persons, natives and foreigners, bodies politic and corporate, Proprietors of the said stock, who should subscribe any share or shares of the said stock, and who, as executors, administrators, successors, or assignees, or by any other lawful title, to be derived from, by, or under the said subscribers, at any time or times thereafter, should have or be entitled to any part, share, or interest of or in the said stock

THIRD WARRANT.

The stock so subscribed, to be under the management of the Corporation thereby established.

so

THIRD WARRANT.

The subscribers to be called by the name of The Royal Bank of Scotland, and by that name to have perpetual succession, and a common Seal, be capable in law to sue and be sued, in any of the Courts within Scotland.

so to be subscribed as aforesaid, should be and be called one Body Politic and Corporate of themselves, in deed and name, by the name of *The Royal Bank of Scotland*; and that such Corporation, and their successors, by the said name, should have perpetual succession, and should and might have and use a common seal, and they and their successors, by the same name, should be able and capable in law, to sue and implead, pursue and defend, answer and be answered, in all or any of his Majesty's Courts within Scotland; and that they and their successors, by the name aforesaid, should and

To purchase lands, &c. in Scotland, and to sell the same.

might be able and capable in law, to have, purchase, receive, possess, enjoy, and retain to them and their successors, lands, rents, tenements, and hereditaments, of what nature, kind, or quality soever, in Scotland only; and also to sell, grant, demise, analzie, or dispone the same: And his Majesty

did

did thereby, for himself, his heirs, and successors, grant unto the said Company of the *Royal Bank of Scotland*, and their successors for ever, full power and liberty to exercise the rights and powers of Banking, in that part of the united kingdom called Scotland only; and in particular to lend to any person or persons, bodies politic or corporate, such sum and sums of money, as they should think fit, at any interest not exceeding lawful interest, on real or personal security; and particularly on pledges of any kind whatsoever, of any goods, wares, merchandises, or other effects whatsoever, in such way and manner as to the said Company should seem proper and convenient; and that the said Company might keep the money or cash of any person or persons, bodies politic and corporate whatsoever, and might borrow, owe, or take up in Scotland, on their bills or notes payable on demand,

THIRD WARRANT.

The *Royal Bank* to have the power of Banking within Scotland.

To lend any sum at any interest not exceeding lawful interest, upon personal and real security, and pledges of any kind.

The *Royal Bank* may keep the cash of other persons, and borrow, owe, and take up money on their bills or notes payable on demand.

THIRD
WARRANT.

to be figned in fuch manner, and by fuch perfons, as the Court of Directors therein after mentioned fhould direct and appoint, or in fuch other manner as the faid Court of Directors fhall think fit, any fum or fums of money whatfoever. And his Majefty did thereby declare, direct, and appoint, That the faid Company fhould not, at

A prohibition to trade with the money or ftock of the Company, in buying or felling wares of any fort.

any time or times, deal or trade, or permit or fuffer any perfon or perfons whatfoever, either in truft or for the benefit of the fame, to deal or trade with any of the ftock, money, or effects, of or any ways belonging to the faid Corporation, in the buying or felling of any goods, wares, or merchandifes whatfoever; provided, that nothing therein contained fhould any

Allowance neverthelefs to deal in bills of exchange, in buying bullion, &c.

ways be conftrued to extend to hinder the faid Corporation from dealing in bills of exchange, or in buying or felling bullion, gold, or filver in Scotland only, or extend to hinder the faid Corporation

poration from selling any goods, wares, merchandises, or effects whatsoever, which should really and *bona fide* be pledged, left, or deposited with the said Corporation, for money lent and advanced thereon, and which should not be redeemed at the time agreed on, or from selling such lands, rents, tenements, or hereditaments, as they should purchase, in virtue of the power thereby given, or from selling such goods as should or might be the produce of lands purchased by the said Corporation. And for the better accomplishment of the ends and intentions proposed by the erecting of the said Corporation, and for making and establishing a continual succession of fit persons to be Managers and Directors of the said Corporation, it was thereby ordained and appointed, That there should be, from time to time, a Governor, Deputy-Governor, nine Ordinary Directors, and nine Extraordinary

THIRD WARRANT.

and selling wares *bona fide* pledged,

and lands, &c. purchased, and the produce thereof.

That there shall be, from time to time, a Governor, Deputy-Governor, nine Ordinary, & nine Extraordinary Directors,

[116]

Third Warrant.

for managing the affairs of the Corporation. The Governor, Deputy-Governor, and nine Ordinary Directors, or any five of them, to be called A Court of Directors.

dinary Directors, to be chosen out of the Members of the said Company; who were to have such qualifications, and to be chosen annually, in the manner and according to the rules and directions therein mentioned; and that five or more should be called *A Court of Directors*, for ordering, managing, and directing all affairs of the said Corporation, in manner above mentioned; and no Governor, Deputy-Governor,

No Governor, Deputy-Governor, or Director, nor any officer or servant under them, shall be capable to act, until they have taken the oaths to the Government.

nor, or Director, or any officer nominated by them, should be capable to sit, vote, or act, or to exercise, use, or discharge any such office, until he had first taken and subscribed the several oaths which then were, or, by any subsequent law, should be directed to be taken by all persons bearing or holding any office, civil or military, under his Majesty, his heirs, and suc-

The Court of Directors may call General Courts of Proprietors, as prescribed;

cessors. And it is thereby further directed, That the said Governor, Deputy-Governor, and Court of Directors,

[117]

tors, should have power and liberty, from time to time, to call General Courts of all the Proprietors, upon giving such notice as therein is prescribed, and there to dispatch any business relating to the government or affairs of the said Corporation, and to remove or displace the said Governor, Deputy-Governor, and any of the Directors, for any misdemeanours or abuse of their office, and elect and chuse new ones in their room, in manner therein mentioned; and to make bye-laws, constitutions, orders, rules, for managing the business of the said Corporation: And that such Court of Directors might appoint a Secretary and all other officers, and displace them as they should see cause. And, for the better carrying on the affairs of the said Corporation, the said Court of Directors, or any nine of them, were directed to inspect, state, and audite the accounts of the Company, and sign and

THIRD WARRANT.

and remove or displace the Governor, Deputy-Governor, & any of the Directors, for misdemeanours, & chuse new ones;

and appoint a Secretary, and other officers, and displace them as they see cause;

and inspect, state, and audite the accounts of the Company.

THIRD WARRANT.

The General Courts may make calls upon the Proprietors;

which are not to exceed 50l. upon the 100l. Capital, and no call to be above 10l. per cent. at a time.

Any perfon neglecting to pay fuch calls fhall not be allowed to transfer their Stock, nor receive any dividends or profits till fuch calls be paid.

and approve thereof, in manner therein directed; and power was thereby given to the General Courts of the faid Company, from time to time, by majority of votes, to make fuch calls upon all and every the Proprietors of the faid Stock and Corporation, as to the majority of fuch General Court fhould feem proper, fo as fuch calls fo to be made do not in the whole exceed fifty pounds upon every hundred pounds of the Subfcribed Capital of the faid Stock, and fo as not above ten pounds in the hundred pounds of the faid Subfcribed Capital of the faid Stock be called at one time; and that fuch calls fhould be paid in by the Proprietors, within the time or times fo limited by fuch General Court; and that no perfon who fhould refufe or neglect to pay in fuch calls, fhould be allowed to transfer or part with any fhare they refpectively had in the faid Stock, nor receive any dividends or profits on account

count thereof, till such calls should by them respectively be paid. And for ascertaining and limiting in what manner, and under what rules the said Capital Stock should and might be assigned and transferred, it was thereby further directed, That there should be forthwith provided and constantly kept in the public office of the said Corporation at Edinburgh, a book or books, wherein all assignments or transfers should be entered, and the said stock should be transferable and transferred, according to the methods and forms therein particularly prescribed and set down; and that any person having any share or interest in the said Stock might dispose and devise the same by his or her last will and testament; and that all such shares or interests in such Stock should be deemed personal estates, and not be liable to any arrestment or attachment. And it was further declared, That the Cashier of the

THIRD WARRANT.

Books for transfers to be kept at Edinburgh.

Any share of the Stock may be disposed of by last will & testament.

The Stock not liable to any arrestment or attachment.

[120]

THIRD WARRANT.

The Cashier of the Corporation, or any other person authorised to receive their proportion of the 10,000 l. annuity.

the said Corporation, or any other person by them lawfully authorised, should, from time to time, receive from the said *Equivalent Company*, or any person by them lawfully authorised, their share and proportion of the said annual sum of Ten thousand pounds payable by virtue of the said recited act of parliament, and dividends, in respect of such of the said Stock of the said *Equivalent Company*, so to be subscribed; and that the General Court of the said Company should, at two terms in the year, declare such dividends as they should think proper to be paid to the respective Proprietors. Provided no dividend should be made but out of the share and interest of the yearly annuity of Ten thousand pounds, and out of the profit arising by borrowing and lending of money, and dealing in the trade and business of Banking; and that such General Court, from time to time, as they should see proper,

The General Court, at two times in every year, is to declare a dividend.

No dividend to be made, but out of their share of the 10,000 l. annuity, and the profits of Banking.

per, might repay all or any part of the said sum of fifty pounds per cent. that should at any time have been called by them upon the Stock of the said Company, as by the said grant or letters patent, passed under the Seal appointed by the Treaty of Union to be kept in Scotland, in place of the Great Seal thereof, relation being thereunto had, doth and may more fully and at large appear. And whereas, by charter or letters patent, passed under the Seal appointed by the Treaty of Union to be kept in Scotland, in place of the Great Seal thereof, and bearing date the first day of November one thousand seven hundred and thirty-eight, reciting to the effect before recited, and also reciting, That the said Company or Corporation of *The Royal Bank of Scotland*, by their most humble application to his late Majesty King George II. of glorious memory, representing, That, in pursu-

THIRD WARRANT.

Calls upon the Stock may be repaid.

Recital of the charter *anno* 1738, confirming and granting new privileges to *The Royal Bank*.

ance

ance of the forefaid letters patent, certain of the Proprietors of the faid *E-
quivalent Company* did fubfcribe parts
and fhares of the faid Stock, for the
purpofes in the faid charter or letters
patent mentioned, to the extent of
One hundred and eleven thoufand
pounds; and that they had for fome
years carried on the bufinefs of Banking, to the great benefit and advantage
of that part of the united kingdom in
general, and in particular to merchants
carrying on and advancing trade: And
further reprefenting, That the annuity to which the Proprietors of the
Equivalent Company, and in confe-
quence the fhares fubfcribed into *The
Royal Bank of Scotland*, being fubject
to redemption, a doubt might arife,
Whether, upon the redemption of the
capital fum of the faid *Equivalent Company* by Parliament, *The Royal Bank
of Scotland* might ceafe and determine; and that it might alfo be doubted,

ed, Whether, in cafe of redemption, the faid fum of One hundred and eleven thoufand pounds muft not be divided amongft the Proprietors, according to their refpective interefts in the faid Stock at the time of redemption: And further reprefenting, That it was found by experience that the then prefent Capital of the faid Bank was not fufficient to anfwer the feveral good ends and purpofes of its erection; and that the Proprietors humbly apprehended, that the addition of any fum not exceeding Forty thoufand pounds to the then prefent Capital, making in the whole the fum of One hundred and fifty-one thoufand pounds, might facilitate their operations, and enable them to be further ufeful in that part of the united kingdom, Whether that addition fhould be made by fubfcribing a further fum of Equivalent Stock, heritable land fecurity, or any other way that fhould appear fafe to the faid Corporation;

THIRD WARRANT.

and, whether the faid fum of 111,000l. muft not be divided amongft the Proprietors.

That the then Capital of the Bank was not fufficient to anfwer the purpofes of their erection; and that the addition of a fum not exceeding 40,000l. to the then Capital, making in the whole 151,000l. might facilitate their operations.

THIRD WARRANT.

That his Majesty would ratify and confirm their privileges, remove all doubts concerning their subsisting, in case of redemption, and enlarge their Capital, by the addition of a sum not exceeding 40,000l.

Corporation; and therefore the said Company or Corporation of *The Royal Bank* most humbly requested, That his said late Majesty would be graciously pleased, by letters patent under the Great Seal of Scotland, to ratify and confirm their privileges, authorities, and rights formerly granted, and to remove all doubts concerning the subsisting of the said Corporation, in case of redemption by Parliament; and to authorise and impower the Proprietors of *The Royal Bank* to enlarge their Capital to any sum not exceeding Forty thousand pounds, by taking in subscriptions of Equivalent Stock, by heritable land security, or by any other way that the Directors of *The Royal Bank*, with consent of their General Court of Proprietors, should judge safe and beneficial to the Bank: Also, that

That the Proprietors might be empowered to take and discharge the Public of the aforesaid 111,000l.

the Proprietors of the said sum of One hundred and eleven thousand pounds Equivalent Stock might be impowered, ed, by authority of a General Court of Proprietors, to take, acquit, and discharge the Public of the aforesaid sum, and to lay out the same in such way and on such security as the Directors aforesaid should judge safe, to the end that a sure and permanent fund might still subsist for the credit of the Bank, and the safety of such as dealt with them. And his said late Majesty being willing to give all proper encouragement to such an undertaking, therefore his Majesty, in compliance with the said request, and by virtue of his prerogative royal, and of his especial grace, certain knowledge, and mere motion, ordained a charter to be made and passed under the Seal appointed by the Treaty of Union to be kept in Scotland, in place of the Great Seal thereof, ratifying and confirming, as his Majesty thereby ratified and confirmed, all the privileges, authorities, and rights, formerly granted to the said Company

THIRD WARRANT.

and lay out the same as the Directors shall judge safe.

The above recital being taken into confideration,

a charter is ordained to pass the Seals of Scotland,

confirming all privileges granted to *The Royal Bank;*

THIRD WARRANT.

and authorising the Governor, Deputy-Governor, & Directors of the said Company, with approbation of a General Court of Proprietors, to enlarge their capital by a sum not exceeding 40,000 l.

Company or Corporation of *The Royal Bank of Scotland*, by the said charter or letters patent, bearing date the thirty-first day of May, in the year one thousand seven hundred and twenty-seven, as aforesaid, in as ample manner and form, as if the same had been all therein particularly mentioned and repeated. And further, his Majesty thereby gave full power and authority to the Governor, Deputy-Governor, and Directors of the said Company of *The Royal Bank of Scotland*, by and with the direction and approbation of a General Court of the Proprietors, to enlarge their then present Capital by a sum not exceeding Forty thousand pounds, and that either by taking subscriptions of other Equivalent Stock not then subscribed into the said Bank, or by taking in subscriptions of certain sums of money upon land security, or any other ways and means that the said

Directors

Directors of *The Royal Bank of Scotland*, by the confent of the faid General Court of Proprietors, fhould judge moft fafe and beneficial to the Corporation of the faid *Royal Bank;* and to that end, his Majefty did thereby authorife and impower the faid Directors to take and receive fuch fubfcriptions, in fuch way and manner as the General Court of the faid Proprietors fhould direct: And for completing the faid additional Stock of Forty thoufand pounds, it fhould and might be lawful to and for the Proprietors of the faid Company of *The Royal Bank*, or the majority of them, in any General Court of the faid Company, to be held as in the faid former charter is mentioned and directed, either to allow the Proprietors of fuch part of the Equivalent Stock, to fubfcribe fuch further or other part of the Stock of the faid Company into the Stock of the faid Company of *The Royal*

THIRD WARRANT.

The Directors to receive fubfcriptions in fuch way as the General Court of Proprietors fhall direct,

for completing the additional ftock of 40,000 l.

To allow the Proprietors of Equivalent Stock to fubfcribe fuch part of the Stock of the faid Company into the Stock of *The Royal Bank*, not exceeding 40,000 l.;

THIRD WARRANT.

Royal Bank, not exceeding in the whole the Sum of Forty thoufand pounds, upon fuch terms and conditions, and at fuch times as the majority of the Proprietors of *The Royal Bank of Scotland*, in fuch General Courts, fhould limit and appoint; or

or to take fuch additional ftock by a voluntary fubfcription, either of money, heritable fecurity, or otherwife.

it fhould and might be lawful for the majority of the Proprietors of the faid *Royal Bank of Scotland*, to take in fuch additional Stock of Forty thoufand pounds by a voluntary fubfcription, either of money upon heritable fecurity, or otherways, and upon fuch terms and conditions, and at fuch times as the majority of the Proprietors of the faid Company of *The Royal Bank of Scotland*, in fuch General Court, fhould limit, direct, and appoint.

The ftock fo fubfcribed, &c. to be under the direction of the Corporation of *The Royal Bank*, as the ftock formerly fubfcribed.

And his Majefty did thereby declare and direct, That fuch Stock of the *Equivalent Company*, fo to be fubfcribed in the terms aforefaid, and fuch fubfcriptions fo to be made in money upon

upon heritable fecurity, or otherways, fhould, from and after fuch fubfcription, be and be under the management, care, and direction of the Corporation or Company of *The Royal Bank* from the time of fuch fubfcription, in the fame way and manner as the Stock formerly fubfcribed was, by the faid former charter or letters patent, directed and appointed; and fhould and might, upon the terms and conditions fo to be limited and appointed, from the time of fuch fubfcription, as aforefaid, have all the fame privileges and liberties as the Proprietors of the firft fubfcribed Stock fhould have or enjoy; and that fuch new Stock, fo to be fubfcribed, fhould be transferable in the fame way and manner, and upon the fame terms and conditions as the then prefent Stock of the faid Company was transferable, by virtue of or under the faid charter of the thirty-firft day of May, in the year one thoufand feven hundred

THIRD WARRANT.

To have the fame privileges as the Proprietors of the firft fubfcribed ftock.

Transferable in the fame way therewith.

R

THIRD WARRANT.

Notwithstanding the Parliament should redeem the Equivalent Stock, the Corporation of *The Royal Bank* should still continue;

hundred and twenty-seven; and the Proprietors of such subscribed Stock should be entitled to have and receive the same, or the like dividends, as should, from time to time, be declared upon the then present Capital of the said Corporation or Company. And his said late Majesty, for the better encouragement of the said *Royal Bank* to proceed in and continue their undertaking of Banking, so much for the benefit of the united kingdom, declared and directed, That, in case the Parliament of Great Britain should, at any time or times, think proper to redeem the said Equivalent Stock, or such part thereof as had been or should be subscribed into the said Company of *The Royal Bank of Scotland*, that the said Corporation or Company of *The Royal Bank of Scotland*, notwithstanding thereof, should and might, after such redemption as aforesaid, continue for ever, and have perpetual succession,

cession, and enjoy all the privileges, benefits, and advantages whatsoever, given and granted to them by the said recited charter and letters patent, except the share or interest in the said annual fund of Ten thousand pounds as aforesaid, as if no such redemption were had or made; and from and after such redemption, all persons having any share or interest, or stock paid into or gained by the said Company, to carry on the trade of the said Company, should be and be deemed Members of the said Company, and be entitled to all the benefits, privileges, and advantages thereof, in proportion to their respective shares and interests in the said money or stock as aforesaid; and the said money or stock so paid, or to be paid, should be assignable or transferable in such and the like manner, *mutatis mutandis*, as the shares in the Capital Stock and yearly Fund were assignable or might be assigned; and that,

THIRD WARRANT.

and enjoy all former privileges, except the share in the annual fund of 10,000l.

After redemption, all persons having interest or stock paid into or gained by the Company, to carry on the trade of the Company, should be deemed Members, and entitled to all advantages thereof;

and the stock so paid, or to be paid, should be transferable, in like manner as the shares in the Capital Stock and yearly fund were then assignable.

THIRD
WARRANT.

The Proprietors in a General Court, or majority of them, impowered to give sufficient authority to their Court of Directors, or such persons as they should nominate, to receive the money payable to the Company upon such redemption as aforesaid, and discharge the same;

and to impower the Court of Directors, from time to time, to lay out the money that should upon redemption be paid, upon such security as the majority of

that, upon such redemption as aforesaid, the Proprietors of the said Stock in the said *Royal Bank*, or the majority of them in a General Court, should and might, and they are thereby impowered and authorised to give sufficient authority to their Court of Directors, or such other person or persons as they should please to nominate and appoint, to receive the money that should be paid or payable to the Company or Corporation, upon such redemption as aforesaid, and give receipts, acquittances, or discharges for for the same; and also, That it should and might be lawful to and for the majority of the said Proprietors of the said Company and Corporation present at their General Court or Courts, and they are thereby impowered and authorised to impower their said Court of Directors, from time to time, to lay out and invest the money that should, upon such redemption, be paid as aforesaid,

aforesaid, upon such security and securities as the said majority of the Proprietors in such General Court should think fit to direct and appoint; and that the interest and produce arising by and from such money, or the securities taken for the same, should be divided to and amongst the Proprietors of the Stock of *The Royal Bank*, in such way and manner, and by such methods, as the said General Court of the said Company or Corporation, or the majority of them, should direct and determine; and that the said money so paid in, and the securities taken for the same, should be under the direction of the General Courts of the Corporation, and the Governor, Deputy-Governor, and Directors of the said Company or Corporation, in the same way and manner, and subject to the same directions and authorities as the then present Capital Stock of the said Corporation or Company were under;

to

THIRD WARRANT.

the Proprietors in such General Court should think fit to appoint.

The Interest arising from such money, or securities for the same, to be divided amongst the Proprietors, in such way as the General Court of the said Company, or majority of them, should direct; and the money so paid, & securities taken for the same, should be under the direction of the General Courts of the Corporation, and Governor, Deputy-Governor, and Directors, in the same way as the then Capital Stock.

THIRD
WARRANT.

That a sure fund might subsist for the credit of the Bank, and security of such as dealt with them;

his Majesty to give such further privileges as he might lawfully grant,

to the end that a sure and permanent fund might subsist for the credit of the said Bank, and security of such as deal with them. And his said late Majesty did thereby, for himself, his heirs, and successors, covenant, grant, and agree to and with the said Corporation or Body Politic, and their successors, That he, his heirs, and successors, should and would, from time to time, and at all times thereafter, upon the humble suit and request of the said Corporation or Body Politic, and their successors, give and grant unto them all such further and other privileges, authorities, matters, and things, for rendering more effectual the said grant, according to the true intent and meaning thereof, which he or they could or might lawfully grant, and as should be reasonably advised and devised by the counsel learned of the said Corporation or Body Politic, for the time being, and should be approved of by the

the Lord Advocate or Solicitor General in Scotland, of his Majesty, his heirs, and successors, on his or their behalf, as by the said grant or letters patent, passed under the Seal appointed by the Treaty of Union to kept in Scotland, in place of the Great Seal thereof, relation being thereunto had, doth and may more fully and at large appear. And considering, That the said Corporation of *The Royal Bank of Scotland* have, by their most humble application to his Majesty, representing, That, since obtaining the foresaid charter erecting *The Royal Bank*, and letters patent afterwards obtained by them, *The Royal Bank of Scotland* have carried on the business of Banking in Scotland very extensively, and much to the benefit of the trade, manufactures, and improvements, in that part of the united kingdom; but that they, by being debarred of the free use and command of the foresaid capital of one

THIRD WARRANT.

Recital of the petition of *The Royal Bank* to his Majesty:

That they have carried on the business of Banking to the benefit of trade, &c.:

THIRD WARRANT.	
That it would be highly advantageous to the country were they allowed the free ufe of faid 111,000l. Equivalent Stock, and enabled to transfer the fame.	one hundred and eleven thoufand pounds of Equivalent Stock, are deprived of the power of fo effectually forwarding the improvement and trade of the country as they could do, were they enabled to transfer their fhares of the faid Equivalent Stock, in the fame manner as they could have done, legally and effectually, in the character of individual Proprietors, before they were incorporated; and therefore praying, That his Majefty would be gracioufly pleafed, by
Praying his Majefty to confirm their privileges;	letters patent under the Great Seal of Scotland, to ratify and confirm their privileges, authorities, and rights, formerly granted by the forefaid charter, erecting *The Royal Bank*, and letters patent afterwards obtained by them;
and to impower the Governor, &c. by authority of a General Court of Proprietors, to transfer their fhares of faid Equivalent Stock,	and to authorife and impower the Governor, Deputy-Governor, and Directors of the faid *Royal Bank*, and their fucceffors in office, by authority of a General Court of Proprietors, to transfer

transfer their shares of the Capital Stock of the *Equivalent Company*, or such part of it as they shall find necessary; and to declare such transfers good and sufficient to the receivers; and that the Governor, Deputy-Governor, and Directors of the said *Royal Bank*, and their successors in office, by authority of a General Court of Proprietors, may be authorised to lay out the money arising from the sale or sales, to be made by them of their shares of the Equivalent Stock, upon lands, bonds, bills, or other good and sufficient security, as shall appear to be most beneficial for the Corporation: And considering such petition has been referred to the Lord Advocate of Scotland for his opinion, what might be reasonable and fitting for his Majesty to do therein; and his Majesty having taken into consideration the said petition, and the report thereupon made by the Lord Advocate of Scotland,

THIRD WARRANT.

and to lay out the money arising therefrom upon lands, bonds, bills, or other good security.

The petition referred to the Lord Advocate of Scotland;

and the same, with the Lord Advocate's report thereon, being taken into consideration,

THIRD WARRANT.

His Majesty ordained a charter to pass the Seals of Scotland,

confirming the privileges formerly granted to the Bank;

Scotland, and being willing to give all proper encouragement to such an undertaking; therefore his Majesty, in compliance with the said request, and by virtue of his prerogative royal, and of his special grace, certain knowledge, and mere motion, ordains a charter to be made and passed under the Seal appointed by the Treaty of Union to be kept in Scotland, in place of the Great Seal thereof, ratifying and confirming, as his Majesty does hereby ratify and confirm all the privileges, authorities, and rights, formerly granted to the said Company or Corporation of *The Royal Bank of Scotland*, by the said charter or letters patent, bearing date the thirty-first day of May, in the year one thousand seven hundred and twenty-seven, erecting the said *Royal Bank*, and by the said letters patent, thereafter granted to the said Bank; bearing date the first day of November, in the year one

one thousand seven hundred and thirty-eight, in as ample manner and form, as if the same were all herein particularly mentioned and repeated. And considering, That, if the Corporation of the said *Royal Bank of Scotland* had power to assign and transfer the aforesaid One hundred and eleven thousand pounds of Equivalent Stock, they would thereby be enabled to carry on the business of Banking to a greater extent, which would be of great advantage to that part of the united kingdom, and would very much promote the trade, manufactures, and improvements of that country, his Majesty hereby gives and grants full power and authority to the Governor, Deputy-Governor, and Directors of the said Company of *The Royal Bank of Scotland*, by and with the direction and approbation of a General Court of the Proprietors thereof, to assign and transfer the said sum of One hundred

THIRD WARRANT.

and further impowering the Governor, &c. with the approbation of a General Court of Proprietors, to transfer the said 111,000l. of Equivalent Stock.

[140]

THIRD WARRANT.

dred and eleven thousand pounds of Equivalent Stock, originally subscribed into the said *Royal Bank*, or such part of it as they shall find necessary, to any person or persons, bodies politic and corporate, notwithstanding that the same is incorporated as the Stock of the said *Royal Bank;* and his Majesty hereby declares, That such transfers or assignments shall be good, valid, and sufficient to such person or persons, bodies politic and corporate, who shall purchase the said Equivalent Stock, or any part thereof. And to remove any doubt as to the subsisting of the said Corporation or Company of *The Royal Bank of Scotland,* after their transferring the said Equivalent Stock, his Majesty hereby declares and directs, that, notwithstanding of such transfers or assignments, of the said Equivalent Stock, the said Corporation or Company of *The Royal Bank of Scotland* shall and may, after such

Such transfers to be good and effectual to the purchasers.

The Corporation of the Bank to subsist notwithstanding of such transfers, such transfers or assignments, as aforesaid, continue for ever, and have perpetual succession, and enjoy all the privileges, benefits, and advantages whatsoever, given and granted to them by the said two recited charters or letters patent, as if no such transfers or assignments had been made; and from and after the making of such transfers or assignments of the said Equivalent Stock, the monies arising therefrom, shall be and be deemed part of the Stock of the said Company or Corporation of *The Royal Bank*, and shall belong to the Proprietors of the said Bank, in proportion to their shares and interest; and shall be assignable or transferable in such and the like manner, *mutatis mutandis*, as the shares of the Capital Stock and yearly Fund are now assignable or may be assigned; and that upon such assigning or transferring of the said sum of One hundred and eleven thousand pounds

of

THIRD WARRANT.

and continue to enjoy all the privileges formerly granted to them.

The money arising from the sale of such Equivalent Stock, shall be deemed part of the Stock of the Bank,

transferable in the same manner as the shares in the Capital Stock and yearly fund are now assignable.

THIRD
WARRANT.

The Proprietors may authorife the Court of Directors to receive the monies arifing from the fales of faid Equivalent Stock.

The Proprietors may authorife the Court of Directors to lay out fuch monies upon fuch fecurities as they fhall think fit.

of Equivalent Stock, or any part thereof, the Proprietors of the faid Stock in *The Royal Bank*, or the majority of them, in a General Court, fhall and may, and they are hereby impowered and authorifed to give fufficient authority to their Court of Directors, or fuch other perfon or perfons as they fhall pleafe to nominate and appoint, to receive the money that fhall be paid or payable to the Company or Corporation, upon fuch transfers or affignments of the faid Equivalent Stock; and alfo that it fhall and may be lawful to and for the majority of the Proprietors of the faid Company and Corporation, prefent at their General Court or Courts, and they are hereby impowered and authorifed to impower their faid Court of Directors, from time to time, to lay out and inveft the money that fhall be received for the faid Equivalent Stock, or any part thereof, upon fuch fecurity and fecurities securities as the said majority of the said Proprietors in such General Courts shall think fit to direct and appoint; and that the interest and produce arising by and from such money, or the securities taken for the same, shall be divided to and amongst the Proprietors of the Stock of *The Royal Bank*, in such way and manner, and by such methods, as the General Court of the said Company and Corporation, or the majority of them, shall direct and determine; and that the said money so paid in, and the securities taken for the same, shall be under the direction of the General Courts of the Corporation, and the Governor, Deputy-Governor, and Directors of the said Company or Corporation, in the same way and manner, and subject to the same rules and directions as the present Capital Stock of the said Corporation or Company is now under; to the end that a sure and permanent fund

THIRD WARRANT.

The interest and produce arising from such monies to be divided amongst the Proprietors, as a General Court shall direct.

The said money, and securities taken for the same, to be subject to the same rules and directions as the present Capital Stock of the Company.

THIRD WARRANT.

Dividends shall only be made out of the interest of the said monies, and from the profits arising from Banking.

These presents to be construed in the most favourable sense for the advantage of the Corporation.

fund may subsist for the credit of the said Bank, and security of such as deal with them. Provided always, That the dividends shall be made to the Proprietors of the said Stock of the said Company, after such assignments or transfers of the said Stock, only out of the interest of the money arising from the sale or sales of the said Equivalent Stock, and out of the profit arising and to arise, by borrowing and lending of money, and dealing in the trade and business of Banking, as aforesaid. And his Majesty does, for himself, his heirs, and successors, grant and declare, That these his letters patent shall be in and by all things valid and effectual in the law, according to the true intent and meaning of the same, and shall be taken, construed, and adjudged, in the most favourable and beneficial sense, for the best advantage of the said Corporation, notwithstanding of any misrecital

cital, defaults, uncertainty, or imperfection, in these his Majesty's letters patent. And his Majesty doth hereby, for himself, his heirs, and successors, covenant, grant, and agree to and with the said Corporation or Body Politic, and their successors, That he, his heirs, and successors, shall and will, from time to time, and at all times hereafter, upon the humble suit and request of the said Corporation or Body Politic, and their successors, give and grant unto them all such further and other privileges, authorities, matters, and things, for rendering more effectual this his grant, according to the true intent and meaning of these presents, which he or they can or may lawfully grant, and as shall be reasonably advised and devised by the counsel learned of the said Corporation or Body Politic for the time being, and shall be approved of by the Lord Advocate or Solicitor General in Scotland

THIRD WARRANT.

His Majesty covenants to give such further privileges as he may lawfully grant;

which shall be devised by their own counsel, and approven of by the Lord Advocate or Solicitor General for Scotland, for the time.

T

THIRD WARRANT.

land of his Majesty, his heirs, and successors, on his or their behalf. And his Majesty does further will and command, That this Charter do pass the Great Seal *per saltum*, without passing any other seal or register. For doing whereof, this shall be, as well to the Directors of his Majesty's Chancery for writing the same, as to the Keeper of the said Seal, for causing the said Seal to be appended thereto, a sufficient warrant.—Given at our Court at St James's this sixteenth day of May one thousand seven hundred and seventy, in the tenth year of our reign.

FOURTH
WARRANT

OF

THE CHARTER

CONFIRMING AND GRANTING

NEW PRIVILEGES

TO THE

Royal Bank of Scotland.

OUR SOVEREIGN LORD confidering,   Preamble. That, by an Act of Parliament made and paffed in the fifth year of the reign of his Majefty King George Firft, entitled, *An Act for fettling certain yearly funds, payable out of the Revenues of* Scotland, *to fatisfy public Debts in* Scotland, *and other ufes mentioned in the Treaty of Union; and to difcharge the Equivalents claimed on behalf of* Scotland,

FOURTH
WARRANT.

Scotland, *in the terms of the said Treaty; and for obviating all future disputes, charges, and expences concerning these Equivalents;* it is enacted,

Reciting the act of Parliament 1719, concerning the L.10,000 Annuity payable to the Creditors of the Public in Scotland.

amongst other things, That yearly, and every year, from the Feast of the Nativity of St John the Baptist, one thousand seven hundred and nineteen years, the full sum of Ten thousand pounds of lawful money of Great Britain shall be a yearly Fund for the particular purposes in that act expressed concerning the same, and shall continue and be payable, in the manner therein particularly expressed for ever, subject nevertheless to redemption by Parliament, according to a *proviso* in the said act contained in that behalf. And it is thereby further enacted,

His Majesty authorised to incorporate the Proprietors of the debts stated to amount to L.248,550:0:9¼.

That it should and might be lawful to and for his Majesty, by letters patent under the Great Seal of Great Britain, to incorporate all and every the Proprietors of the debts and sums of money,

money, stated to amount to the principal sum of Two hundred and thirty thousand three hundred and eight pounds nine shillings ten pence and five sixth parts of a penny, due to the creditors of the public in Scotland, on the twenty-fourth day of June one thousand seven hundred and fourteen years, and Eighteen thousand two hundred and forty-one pounds ten shillings ten pence and two thirds of a penny, stated due to William Paterson, Esq. making together Two hundred and forty-eight thousand five hundred and fifty pounds and nine pence halfpenny, to be one Body Politic and Corporate, by such name as his Majesty should think most proper, and that by such name the said Corporation should have perpetual succession, subject to such redemption as in the said act is appointed; with such powers to do and perform all matters appertaining to them to do and perform,
touching

FOURTH WARRANT.

due to the creditors of the public in Scotland,

by such name as he should think fit.

[150]

FOURTH WARRANT.

touching or concerning the said capital sums, and the said yearly fund payable in respect thereof, as his Majesty by the same letters patent should think fit to grant. And it was thereby enacted, That the said capital sum,

And the said L..248,550 : 0 : 9¼, should be the Capital or Joint Stock of the Corporation,

amounting to Two hundred forty-eight thousand five hundred and fifty pounds and nine pence halfpenny, should be, and be deemed to be, the Capital or Joint Stock of the said Corporation; and that the shares of the Members of and in the same should be from time to time assignable, transferable, and deviseable, in such manner as his Majesty by such letters patent should prescribe and appoint, until the redemption thereof; and that

and be deemed personal or moveable estates,

the same should be deemed to be personal or moveable estates, and should go to executors or administrators, and

not liable to arrestments or attachments.

should not be liable to any arrestments or attachments that should be laid thereon. And it is thereby enacted, That

[151]

FOURTH WARRANT.

That all and every the Members of the said Corporation should have and be entitled to an annuity or yearly sum, in proportion to his or their share in the said capital sum and stock of Two hundred and forty-eight thousand five hundred and fifty pounds and nine pence halfpenny; and the said annuity should be paid in the manner in the said act mentioned, and to and for no other use, intent, or purpose whatsoever. And it was further enacted, That, above the said annuity of Ten thousand pounds per annum, there should be paid to the said Corporation and their successors, until the redemption of such annual sum, the further annual sum of Six hundred pounds per annum, towards the necessary charges of the management thereof, as in and by the said act of Parliament, amongst other clauses and things therein contained, relation being thereunto had, doth more fully

L. 600 per annum to be paid to the Corporation for charges of management.

and

[152]

FOURTH WARRANT.

Recital of the charter erecting the Proprietors of the forefaid debt into a Corporation, by the name of the EQUIVALENT COMPANY.

and at large appear. And confidering, That his faid Majefty King George the Firft, of glorious memory, by his letters patent, bearing date at Weftminfter, the twenty-firft day of November, in the eleventh year of his reign, in purfuance of the faid act of Parliament, and by virtue of his prerogative royal, and likewife of his efpecial grace, certain knowledge, and mere motion, did give, grant, make, ordain, declare, appoint, and eftablifh, That all and every perfon or perfons, natives and foreigners, bodies politic and corporate, who then were Proprietors of the debts and fums of money fo ftated to amount to Two hundred forty-eight thoufand five hundred and fifty pounds and nine pence halfpenny, or who, by any lawful title, derived, or to be derived, from, by, or under the faid Proprietors at any time thereafter, fhould have, and be entitled to any part, fhare, or intereft therein, fhould should be, and be called, one Body Politic and Corporate of themselves, in deed and name, by the name of the EQUIVALENT COMPANY; and that such Corporation, and their successors, should have perpetual succession, subject to such redemption as is therein mentioned, and should and might have and use a common seal, and should, by that name, be capable to sue and be sued; and that the sum of Two hundred forty-eight thousand five hundred and fifty pounds and nine pence halfpenny, should be accepted, deemed, and esteemed the Capital or Joint Stock of the said Corporation, and all the Proprietors of such stock should be Members of the said Corporation; and that the said annuity of Ten thousand pounds per annum should be paid to the said Company or their Cashier, to be divided and distributed to and amongst the several Proprietors, in proportion to their respective

FOURTH WARRANT.

The foresaid L.248,550 : 0 : 9½ to be the Capital or Joint Stock of the EQUIVALENT COMPANY:

And the annuity of L.10,000, payable to the Company or their Cashier, to be divided amongst the Proprietors, according to their shares in the stock.

[154]

FOURTH WARRANT.

spective shares in the said Capital or Joint Stock. And that his said Majesty did thereby further order and direct, limit, and appoint, That the said stock should be transferable and assignable; and all assignments or transfers of the said capital stock, or yearly fund, or any part thereof, should be in the manner, and according to the methods thereby directed: And likewise appointed, That the said annual sum of Six hundred pounds for charges of management, should be paid to the said Corporation, or such as they should authorise, under their common seal, to receive the same, for the uses of the said Corporation, as by the said grant or letters patent, passed under the Great Seal of Great Britain, relation being thereunto had, doth and may more fully and at large appear. And whereas by charter or letters patent, passed under the Seal appointed by the Treaty of Union to be kept in Scotland,

The stock of the Company to be transferable.

The L.600 is payable to the EQUIVALENT COMPANY, or any person to be appointed by them, under their seal, to receive the same.

Recital of the Charter granting the power of Banking, &c. in Scotland, upon petition of the EQUIVALENT COMPANY,

Scotland, in place of the Great Seal thereof, and bearing date the thirty-firſt day of May one thouſand ſeven hundred and twenty-ſeven, reciting to the effect before recited, and alſo reciting that the ſaid Corporation of the *Equivalent Company*, by their moſt humble application to his ſaid late Majeſty, requeſted, That he would be graciouſly pleaſed, by letters patent under the Great Seal of Scotland, to enable ſuch of the Proprietors of the ſaid Corporation as ſhould ſubſcribe their ſtock for that purpoſe, to have the power of Banking in Scotland only, with liberty to borrow and lend upon ſecurity there; that the ſaid Corporation might be for that purpoſe impowered to take ſubſcriptions at Edinburgh from their Members, for ſuch ſhare of the ſtock as they ſhall incline to ſubject to ſuch Trade or Banking, under ſuch regulations as they by bye-laws ſhould appoint; and that ſuch ſubſcribed

FOURTH WARRANT.

to ſuch of the Members as ſhould ſubſcribe their ſtock for that purpoſe.

FOURTH WARRANT.

Such subscribed stock only to be subject to the transactions of Banking, & thereafter to be transferable from the other stock of the EQUIVALENT COMPANY, *and at Edinburgh only.*

bed stock only should be affected by the transactions relating to Banking, and (after being so subscribed) become transferable from the other stock of the Company, and at Edinburgh only; and would erect such subscribers into a Corporation for that purpose; and that such power of Banking, so established, would manifestly tend to the great benefit and advantage of that part of the kingdom; his Majesty, being willing to give all proper encouragement to such an undertaking, therefore his said Majesty, in compliance with the said request, and by virtue of his prerogative royal, and of his especial grace, certain knowledge, and mere motion, and for the benefit of his subjects in that part of

A Charter ordained to pass the Seals of Scotland,

the united kingdoms, ordained a charter to be made and passed under the Seal appointed by the Treaty of Union to be kept in Scotland, in place of the Great Seal thereof, nominating, authorising,

[157]

authorising, and appointing, as his Majesty thereby nominated, authorised, and appointed the persons therein named, or any three of them, in such way and manner as they, or the majority of them, should direct, to take and receive at Edinburgh all such voluntary subscriptions as should be made, on or before the twenty-ninth day of September one thousand seven hundred and twenty-seven years, by any person or persons, Members or Proprietors of the said *Equivalent Company*, who had, or should have credit for stock in the books of the said Company at Edinburgh, at the time of such subscription, of all or any of such part or share of the stock of the said Equivalent Company, as he, she, or they, should think proper, for and towards raising a fund for the more effectually carrying on the said trade and business of Banking there, and the uses therein after mentioned; which said subscriptions

FOURTH WARRANT.

authorising the Directors of the said EQUIVALENT COMPANY, or any three of them, in such way as the majority of them shall direct, to receive at Edinburgh all such voluntary subscriptions as should be made on or before the 29th day of September 1727, by the Proprietors of the said Company.

FOURTH WARRANT.

Which subscriptions are to be entered in books to be kept for that purpose.

The stock so subscribed, to be under the management of the Corporation thereby established.

tions the said Proprietors were thereby impowered to make, and the same should be fairly entered in books to be kept for that purpose; and the then present stock of the said Equivalent Company, so to be subscribed as aforesaid, should, from and after the time of such subscription, be under the order, management, and direction of the Company thereby established. And his Majesty, by virtue of the said prerogative, and likewise of his especial grace, certain knowledge, and mere motion, gave, granted, made, ordained, constituted, declared, appointed, and established, That all and every person and persons, natives and foreigners, bodies politic and corporate, Proprietors of the said stock, who should subscribe any share or shares of the said stock, and who, as executors, administrators, successors, or assignees, or by any other lawful title, to be derived from, by, or under the said subscribers,

bers, at any time or times thereafter, should have or be entitled to any part, share, or interest of or in the said stock so to be subscribed as aforesaid, should be and be called one Body Politic and Corporate of themselves, in deed and name, by the name of *The Royal Bank of Scotland*; and that such Corporation, and their successors, by the said name, should have perpetual succession, and should and might have and use a common seal, and they and their successors, by the same name, should be able and capable in law, to sue and implead, pursue and defend, answer and be answered, in all or any of his Majesty's Courts within Scotland; and that they and their successors, by the name aforesaid, should and might be able and capable in law, to have, purchase, receive, possess, enjoy, and retain to them and their successors, lands, rents, tenements, and hereditaments, of what kind, nature, or quality

FOURTH WARRANT.

The subscribers to be called by the name of *The Royal Bank of Scotland*, and by that name to have perpetual succession, and a common Seal, be capable in law to sue and be sued, in any of the Courts within Scotland.

To purchase lands, &c. in Scotland, and to sell the same.

FOURTH WARRANT.

The Royal Bank to have the power of Banking within Scotland.

To lend any sum at any interest not exceeding lawful interest, upon personal and real security, and pledges of any kind.

The Royal Bank may keep the cash of other persons, and borrow, owe, and take up mo-

quality soever, in Scotland only; and also to sell, grant, demise, analzie, or dispone the same: And his Majesty did thereby, for himself, his heirs, and successors, grant unto the said Company of the *Royal Bank of Scotland*, and their successors for ever, full power and liberty to exercise the rights and powers of Banking, in that part of the united kingdom called Scotland only; and in particular to lend to any person or persons, bodies politic or corporate, such sum and sums of money, as they should think fit, at any interest not exceeding lawful interest, on real or personal security; and particularly on pledges of any kind whatsoever, of any goods, wares, merchandises, or other effects whatsoever, in such way and manner as to the said Company should seem proper and convenient; and that the said Company might keep the money or cash of any person or persons, bodies politic and corporate

corporate whatsoever, and may borrow, owe, or take up in Scotland, on their bills or notes payable on demand, to be signed in such manner, and by such persons, as the Court of Directors therein after mentioned should direct and appoint, or in such other manner as the said Court of Directors shall think fit, any sum or sums of money whatsoever. And his Majesty did thereby declare, direct, and appoint, That the said Company should not, at any time or times, deal or trade, or permit or suffer any person or persons whatsoever, either in trust or for the benefit of the same, to deal or trade with any of the stock, money, or effects, of or any ways belonging to the said Corporation, in the buying or selling of any goods, wares, or merchandises whatsoever; provided, that nothing therein contained should any ways be construed to extend to hinder the said Corporation from dealing in

FOURTH WARRANT.

ney on their bills or notes payable on demand.

A prohibition to trade with the money or stock of the Company, in buying or selling wares of any sort.

Allowance nevertheless to deal in bills of exchange, in buying bullion, &c.

bills

_{FOURTH}
_{WARRANT,}

_{and selling wares}
_{bona fide pledged,}

_{and lands, &c.}
_{purchased, and the}
_{produce thereof.}

bills of exchange, or in buying or selling bullion, gold, or silver in Scotland only, or extend to hinder the said Corporation from selling any goods, wares, merchandises, or effects whatsoever, which should really and *bona fide* be pledged, left, or deposited with the said Corporation, for money lent and advanced thereon, and which should not be redeemed at the time agreed on, or from selling such lands, rents, tenements, or hereditaments, as they should purchase, in virtue of the power thereby given, or from selling such goods as should or might be the produce of lands purchased by the said Corporation. And for the better accomplishment of the ends and intentions proposed by the erecting of the said Corporation, and for making and establishing a continual succession of fit persons to be Managers and Directors of the said Corporation, it was thereby ordained and appointed, That there

should

should be, from time to time, a Governor, Deputy-Governor, nine Ordinary Directors, and nine Extraordinary Directors, to be chosen out of the Members of the said Company; who were to have such qualifications, and to be chosen annually, in the manner and according to the rules and directions therein mentioned; and that five or more should be called *A Court of Directors*, for ordering, managing, and directing all affairs of the said Corporation, in manner above mentioned; and no Governor, Deputy-Governor, or Director, or any officer nominated by them, should be capable to sit, vote, or act, or to exercise, use, or discharge any such office, until he had first taken and subscribed the several oaths which then were, or, by any subsequent law, should be directed to be taken by all persons bearing or holding any office, civil or military, under his Majesty, his heirs, and successors.

FOURTH WARRANT.

That there shall be, from time to time, a Governor, Deputy-Governor, nine Ordinary, & nine Extraordinary Directors, for managing the affairs of the Corporation. The Governor, Deputy-Governor, and nine Ordinary Directors, or any five of them, to be called *A Court of Directors*.

No Governor, Deputy-Governor, or Director, nor any officer or servant under them, shall be capable to act, until they have taken the oaths to the Government.

cessors. And it is thereby further directed, That the said Governor, Deputy-Governor, and Court of Directors, or, in their default, any nine of the Proprietors of the shares of Stock therein specified, should have power and liberty, from time to time, to call General Courts of all the Proprietors, upon giving such notice as therein is prescribed, and there to dispatch any business relating to the government or affairs of the said Corporation, and to remove or displace the said Governor, Deputy-Governor, and any of the Directors, for any misdemeanours or abuse of their office, and elect and chuse new ones in their room, in manner therein mentioned; and to make bye-laws, constitutions, orders, rules, for managing the business of the said Corporation: And that such Court of Directors might appoint a Secretary and all other officers, and displace them as they should see cause. And, for the better

Marginalia:
FOURTH WARRANT.
The Court of Directors may call General Courts of Proprietors, as prescribed; or, in their default, any nine of the Proprietors;

and remove or displace the Governor, Deputy-Governor, & any of the Directors, for misdemeanours, & chuse new ones;

and appoint a Secretary, and other officers, and displace them as they see cause;

better carrying on the affairs of the said Corporation, the said Court of Directors, or any nine of them, were directed to inspect, state, and audite the accounts of the Company, and sign and approve thereof, in manner therein directed; and power was thereby given to the General Courts of the said Company, from time to time, by majority of votes, to make such calls upon all and every the Proprietors of the said Stock and Corporation, as to the majority of such General Court should seem proper, so as such calls so to be made do not in the whole exceed fifty pounds upon every hundred pounds of the Subscribed Capital of the said Stock, and so as not above ten pounds in the hundred pounds of the said Subscribed Capital of the said Stock be called at one time; and that such calls should be paid in by the Proprietors, within the time or times so limited by such General Court; and that no person

FOURTH WARRANT.

and inspect, state, and audite the accounts of the Company.

The General Courts may make calls upon the Proprietors;

which are not to exceed 50l. upon the 100l. Capital, and no call to be above 10l. per cent. at a time.

FOURTH WARRANT.

Any person neglecting to pay such calls shall not be allowed to transfer their Stock, nor receive any dividends or profits till such calls be paid.

person who should refuse or neglect to pay in such calls, should be allowed to transfer or part with any share they respectively had in the said Stock, nor receive any dividends or profits on account thereof, till such calls should by them respectively be paid. And for ascertaining and limiting in what manner, and under what rules the said Capital Stock should and might be assigned and transferred, it was thereby further directed, That there should be forthwith provided and constantly kept in the public office of the said Corporation at Edinburgh, a book or books, wherein all assignments or transfers should be entered, and the said stock should be transferable and transferred, according to the methods and forms therein particularly prescribed and set down; and that any person having any share or interest in the said Stock might dispose and devise the same by his or her last will and testament; and

Books for transfers to be kept at Edinburgh.

Any share of the Stock may be disposed of by last will & testament.

[167]

and that all such shares or interests in such Stock should be deemed personal estates, and not be liable to any arrestment or attachment. And it was further declared, That the Cashier of the said Corporation, or any other person by them lawfully authorised, should, from time to time, receive from the said *Equivalent Company*, or any person by them lawfully authorised, their share and proportion of the said annual sum of Ten thousand pounds payable by virtue of the said recited act of parliament, and dividends, in respect of such of the said Stock of the said *Equivalent Company*, so to be subscribed; and that the General Court of the said Company should, at two terms in the year, declare such dividends as they should think proper to be paid to the respective Proprietors. Provided no dividend should be made but out of the share and interest of the yearly annuity of Ten thousand pounds, and out

FOURTH WARRANT.

The Stock not liable to any arrestment or attachment.

The Cashier of the Corporation, or any other person authorised to receive their proportion of the 10,000 l. annuity.

The General Court, at two times in every year, is to declare a dividend.

No dividend to be made, but out of their share of the 10,000 l. annuity, and the profits of Banking.

[168]

FOURTH WARRANT.

out of the profit arifing by borrowing and lending of money, and dealing in the trade and bufinefs of Banking; and that fuch General Court, from time to time, as they fhould fee proper, might repay all or any part of the faid fum of fifty pounds per cent. that fhould at any time have been called by them upon the Stock of the faid Company, as by the faid grant or letters patent, paffed under the Seal appointed by the Treaty of Union to be kept in Scotland, in place of the Great Seal thereof, relation being thereunto had, doth and may more fully and at large appear. And whereas, by charter or letters patent, paffed under the Seal appointed by the Treaty of Union to be kept in Scotland, in place of the Great Seal thereof, and bearing date the firft day of November in the year one thoufand feven hundred and thirty-eight, reciting to the effect before recited, and alfo reciting, That the

Calls upon the Stock may be repaid.

Recital of the charter *anno* 1738, confirming and granting new privileges to *The Royal Bank.*

FOURTH WARRANT.

the said Company or Corporation of *The Royal Bank of Scotland*, by their most humble application to his late Majesty King George II. of glorious memory, representing, That, in pursuance of the foresaid letters patent, certain of the Proprietors of the said *Equivalent Company* did subscribe parts and shares of the said Stock, for the purposes in the said charter or letters patent mentioned, to the extent of One hundred and eleven thousand pounds; and that they had for some years carried on the business of Banking, to the great benefit and advantage of that part of the united kingdom in general, and in particular to merchants carrying on and advancing trade: And further representing, That the annuity to which the Proprietors of the *Equivalent Company*, and in consequence the shares subscribed into *The Royal Bank of Scotland*, being subject to redemption, a doubt might arise,

That in pursuance of the said letters patent, Proprietors of the *Equivalent Company* did subscribe Stock to the extent of 111,000l.

That the annuity payable to the Proprietors of *Equivalent*, and shares subscribed into *The Royal Bank*, being subject to redemption, a doubt might arise, Whether, upon such redemption, *The Royal Bank* might cease;

Y   Whether

[170]

FOURTH WARRANT.

and, whether the said sum of 111,600l. must not be divided amongst the Proprietors.

That the then Capital of the Bank was not sufficient to answer the purposes of their erection; and that the addition of a sum not exceeding 40,000l. to the then Capital, making in the whole 151,000l. might facilitate their operations.

Whether, upon the redemption of the capital sum of the said *Equivalent Company* by Parliament, *The Royal Bank of Scotland* might cease and determine; and that it might also be doubted, Whether, in case of redemption, the said sum of One hundred and eleven thousand pounds must not be divided amongst the Proprietors, according to their respective interests in the said Stock at the time of redemption: And further representing, That it was found by experience that the then present Capital of the said Bank was not sufficient to answer the several good ends and purposes of its erection; and that the Proprietors humbly apprehended, that the addition of any sum not exceeding Forty thousand pounds to the then present Capital, making in the whole the sum of One hundred and fifty-one thousand pounds, might facilitate their operations, and enable them to be further useful in that part

of

of the united kingdom, Whether that addition should be made by subscribing a further sum of Equivalent Stock, heritable land security, or any other way that should appear safe to the said Corporation; and therefore the said Company or Corporation of *The Royal Bank* most humbly requested, That his said late Majesty would be graciously pleased, by letters patent under the Great Seal of Scotland, to ratify and confirm their privileges, authorities, and rights formerly granted, and to remove all doubts concerning the subsisting of the said Corporation, in case of redemption by Parliament; and to authorise and impower the Proprietors of *The Royal Bank* to enlarge their Capital to any sum not exceeding Forty thousand pounds, by taking in subscriptions of Equivalent Stock, by heritable land security, or by any other way that the Directors of *The Royal Bank*, with consent of their General Court

FOURTH WARRANT.

That his Majesty would ratify and confirm their privileges, remove all doubts concerning their subsisting, in case of redemption, and enlarge their Capital, by the addition of a sum not exceeding 40,000l.

FOURTH
WARRANT.

That the Proprietors might be empowered to take and discharge the Public of the aforesaid 111,000l. and lay out the same as the Directors shall judge safe.

The above recital being taken into consideration,

a charter is ordained to pass the Seals of Scotland,

Court of Proprietors, should judge safe and beneficial to the Bank: Also, that the Proprietors of the said sum of One hundred and eleven thousand pounds Equivalent Stock might be impowered, by authority of a General Court of Proprietors, to take, acquit, and discharge the Public of the aforesaid sum, and to lay out the same in such way and on such security as the Directors aforesaid should judge safe, to the end that a sure and permanent fund might still subsist for the credit of the Bank, and the safety of such as dealt with them. And his said late Majesty being willing to give all proper encouragement to such an undertaking, therefore his Majesty, in compliance with the said request, and by virtue of his prerogative royal, and of his especial grace, certain knowledge, and mere motion, ordained a charter to be made and passed under the Seal appointed by the Treaty of Union to be kept in Scotland,

land, in place of the Great Seal thereof, ratifying and confirming, as his Majesty thereby ratified and confirmed, all the privileges, authorities, and rights, formerly granted to the Company or Corporation of *The Royal Bank of Scotland*, by the said charter or letters patent, bearing date the thirty-first day of May, in the year one thousand seven hundred and twenty-seven, as aforesaid, in as ample manner and form, as if the same had been all therein particularly mentioned and repeated, And further, his Majesty thereby gave full power and authority to the Governor, Deputy-Governor, and Directors of the said Company of *The Royal Bank of Scotland*, by and with the direction and approbation of a General Court of the Proprietors, to enlarge their then present Capital to any sum not exceeding Forty thousand pounds, and that either by taking subscriptions of other

FOURTH WARRANT.

confirming all privileges granted to *The Royal Bank;*

and authorising the Governor, Deputy-Governor, & Directors of the said Company, with approbation of a General Court of Proprietors, to enlarge their capital by a sum not exceeding 40,000 l.

FOURTH
WARRANT.

The Directors to receive subscriptions in such way as the General Court of Proprietors shall direct,

for completing the additional stock of 40,000 l.

other Equivalent Stock not then subscribed into the said Bank, or by taking in subscriptions of certain sums of money upon land security, or any other ways and means that the said Directors of *The Royal Bank of Scotland*, by the consent of the said General Court of Proprietors, should judge most safe and beneficial to the Corporation of the said *Royal Bank;* and to that end, his Majesty did thereby authorise and impower the said Directors to take and receive such subscriptions, in such way and manner as the General Court of the said Proprietors should direct: And for completing the said additional Stock of Forty thousand pounds, it should and might be lawful to and for the Proprietors of the said Company of *The Royal Bank*, or the majority of them, in any General Court of the said Company, to be held as in the said former charter is mentioned and directed,

rected, either to allow the Proprietors of such part of the Equivalent Stock, to subscribe such further or other part of the Stock of the said Company into the Stock of the said Company of *The Royal Bank*, not exceeding in the whole the Sum of Forty thousand pounds, upon such terms and conditions, and at such times as the majority of the Proprietors of *The Royal Bank of Scotland*, in such General Courts, should limit and appoint; or it should and might be lawful for the majority of the Proprietors of the said *Royal Bank of Scotland*, to take in such additional Stock of Forty thousand pounds by a voluntary subscription, either of money upon heritable security, or otherways, and upon such terms and conditions, and at such times as the majority of the Proprietors of the said Company of *The Royal Bank of Scotland*, in such General Court, should limit, direct, and appoint.

And

FOURTH WARRANT.

To allow the Proprietors of Equivalent Stock to subscribe such part of the Stock of the said Company into the Stock of *The Royal Bank*, not exceeding 40,000 l.;

or to take such additional stock by a voluntary subscription, either of money, heritable security, or otherwise.

FOURTH WARRANT.

The stock so subscribed, &c. to be under the direction of the Corporation of *The Royal Bank*, as the stock formerly subscribed.

And his Majesty did thereby declare and direct, That such Stock of the *Equivalent Company*, so to be subscribed in the terms aforesaid, and such subscriptions so to be made in money upon heritable security, or otherways, should, from and after such subscription, be under the management, care, and direction of the Corporation or Company of *The Royal Bank* from the time of such subscription, in the same way and manner as the Stock formerly subscribed was, by the said former charter or letters patent, directed and appointed; and should and might, upon the terms and conditions so to be limited and appointed, from the time of such subscription, as aforesaid, have all the same privileges and liberties as the Proprietors of the first subscribed Stock should have or enjoy; and that such new Stock, so to be subscribed, should be transferable in the same way and manner, and upon the same

To have the same privileges as the Proprietors of the first subscribed stock.

same terms and conditions as the then present Stock of the said Company was transferable, by virtue of or under the said charter of the thirty-firſt day of May, in the year one thouſand ſeven hundred and twenty-ſeven; and the Proprietors of ſuch ſubſcribed Stock ſhould be entitled to have and receive the ſame, or the like dividends, as ſhould, from time to time, be declared upon the then preſent Capital of the ſaid Corporation or Company. And his ſaid late Majeſty, for the better encouragement of the ſaid *Royal Bank* to proceed in and continue their undertaking of Banking, ſo much for the benefit of the ſaid united kingdom, declared and directed, That, in caſe the Parliament of Great Britain ſhould, at any time or times, think proper to redeem the ſaid Equivalent Stock, or ſuch part thereof as had been or ſhould be ſubſcribed into the ſaid Company of *The Royal Bank of Scotland*, that the

FOURTH WARRANT.

Transferable in the ſame way therewith.

Notwithſtanding the Parliament ſhould redeem the Equivalent Stock, the Corporation of *The Royal Bank* ſhould ſtill continue;

FOURTH
WARRANT.

and enjoy all former privileges, except the share in the annual fund of 10,000l.

After redemption, all persons having interest or stock paid into or gained by the Company, to carry on the trade of the Company, should be deemed Members, and entitled to all advantages thereof;

the said Corporation or Company of *The Royal Bank of Scotland*, notwithstanding thereof, should and might, after such redemption as aforesaid, continue for ever, and have perpetual succession, and enjoy all the privileges, benefits, and advantages whatsoever, given and granted to them by the said recited charter and letters patent, except the share or interest in the said annual fund of Ten thousand pounds as aforesaid, as if no such redemption were had or made; and from and after such redemption, all persons having any share or interest, or stock paid into or gained by the said Company, to carry on the trade of the said Company, should be and be deemed Members of the said Company, and be entitled to all the benefits, privileges, and advantages thereof, in proportion to their respective shares and interests in the said money or stock as aforesaid; and the said money or stock so paid, or to be be paid, should be assignable or transferable in such and the like manner, *mutatis mutandis*, as the shares in the Capital Stock and yearly Fund were assignable or might be assigned; and that, upon such redemption as aforesaid, the Proprietors of the said Stock in the said *Royal Bank*, or the majority of them in a General Court, should and might, and they are thereby impowered and authorised to give sufficient authority to their Court of Directors, or such other person or persons as they should please to nominate and appoint, to receive the money that should be paid or payable to the Company or Corporation, upon such redemption as aforesaid, and give receipts, acquittances, or discharges for the same; and also, That it should and might be lawful to and for the majority of the said Proprietors of the said Company and Corporation present at their General Court or Courts,

and

FOURTH WARRANT.

and the stock so paid, or to be paid, should be transferable, in like manner as the shares in the Capital Stock and yearly fund were then assignable.

The Proprietors in a General Court, or majority of them, impowered to give sufficient authority to their Court of Directors, or such persons as they should nominate, to receive the money payable to the Company upon such redemption as aforesaid, and discharge the same;

[180]

<small>FOURTH WARRANT.</small>

and they are thereby impowered and authorised to impower their said Court of Directors, from time to time, to lay out and invest the money that should, upon such redemption, be paid as aforesaid, upon such security and securities as the said majority of the Proprietors in such General Court should think fit to direct and appoint; and the interest and produce arising by and from such money, or the securities taken for the same, should be divided to and amongst the Proprietors of the said Stock of *The Royal Bank*, in such way and manner, and by such methods, as the said General Court of the said Company or Corporation, or the majority of them, should direct and determine; and that the said money so paid in, and the securities taken for the same, should be under the direction of the General Courts of the Corporation, and the Governor, Deputy-Governor, and Directors of the said Company

<small>and to impower the Court of Directors, from time to time, to lay out the money that should upon redemption be paid, upon such security as the majority of the Proprietors in such General Court should think fit to appoint.</small>

<small>The interest arising from such money, or securities for the same, to be divided amongst the Proprietors, in such way as the General Court of the said Company, or majority of them, should direct; and the money so paid, & securities taken for the same, should be under the direction of the General Courts of the Corporation, and Governor, Deputy-Governor, and Directors, in the same way as the then Capital Stock.</small>

Company or Corporation, in the same way and manner, and subject to the same directions and authorities as the then present Capital Stock of the said Corporation or Company were under; to the end that a sure and permanent fund might subsist for the credit of the said Bank, and security of such as dealt with them. And his said late Majesty did thereby, for himself, his heirs, and successors, covenant, grant, and agree to and with the said Corporation or Body Politic, and their successors, That he, his heirs, and successors, should and would, from time to time, and at all times thereafter, upon the humble suit and request of the said Corporation or Body Politic, and their successors, give and grant unto them all such further and other privileges, and authorities, matters, and things, for rendering more effectual the said grant, according to the true intent and meaning thereof, which he or they could or

might

FOURTH WARRANT.

That a sure fund might subsist for the credit of the Bank, and security of such as dealt with them;

his Majesty to give such further privileges as he might lawfully grant, might lawfully grant, and as should be reasonably advised and devised by the counsel learned of the said Corporation or Body Politic, for the time being, and should be approved of by the Lord Advocate or Solicitor General in Scotland, of his Majesty, his heirs, and successors, on his or their behalf, as by the said grant or letters patent, passed under the Seal appointed by the Treaty of Union to be kept in Scotland, in place of the Great Seal thereof, relation being thereunto had, doth and may more fully and at large appear. And whereas our Sovereign Lord, by charter or letters patent under the Seal appointed by the Treaty of Union to be kept in Scotland, in place of the Great Seal thereof, and bearing date the sixteenth day of May one thousand seven hundred and seventy, reciting to the effect before recited; and also reciting, That the said Company, since obtaining the foresaid charter

FOURTH WARRANT.

Recital of the petition of *The Royal Bank* to his Majesty,

charter erecting *The Royal Bank*, and letters patent afterwards obtained by them, *The Royal Bank of Scotland* have carried on the bufinefs of Banking in Scotland very extenfively, and much to the benefit of the trade, manufactures, and improvements, in that part of the united kingdom; but that they, by being debarred of the free ufe and command of the forefaid capital of one hundred and eleven thoufand pounds of Equivalent Stock, are deprived of the power of fo effectually forwarding the improvement and trade of the country as they could do, were they enabled to transfer their fhares of the faid Equivalent Stock, in the fame manner as they could have done, legally and effectually, in the character of individual Proprietors, before they were incorporated; and therefore praying, That his Majefty would be gracioufly pleafed, by letters patent under the Great Seal of Scotland,

FOURTH WARRANT.

That they have carried on the bufinefs of Banking to the benefit of trade, &c.:

That it would be highly advantageous to the country were they allowed the free ufe of faid 111,000l. Equivalent Stock, and enabled to transfer the fame.

Praying his Majefty to confirm their privileges;

FOURTH WARRANT.

and to impower the Governor, &c. by authority of a General Court of Proprietors, to transfer their shares of said Equivalent Stock,

Scotland, to ratify and confirm their privileges, authorities, and rights, formerly granted by the foresaid charter, erecting *The Royal Bank*, and letters patent afterwards obtained by them; and to authorise and impower the Governor, Deputy-Governor, and Directors of the said *Royal Bank*, and their successors in office, by authority of a General Court of Proprietors, to transfer their shares of the Capital Stock of the *Equivalent Company*, or such part of it as they should find necessary; and to declare such transfers good and sufficient to the receivers; and that the Governor, Deputy-Governor, and Directors of the said *Royal Bank*, and their successors in office, by authority of a General Court of

and to lay out the money arising therefrom upon lands, bonds, bills, or other good security.

Proprietors, might be authorised to lay out the money arising from the sale or sales, to be made by them of their shares of the Equivalent Stock, upon lands, bonds, bills, or other good and sufficient

sufficient security, as shall appear to be most beneficial for the Corporation; therefore his Majesty ordained a charter to be made and passed under the Seal appointed by the Treaty of Union to be kept in Scotland, in place of the Great Seal thereof, ratifying and confirming, as his Majesty thereby ratified and confirmed all the privileges, authorities, and rights, formerly granted to the said Company or Corporation of *The Royal Bank of Scotland*, by the said charter or letters patent, bearing date the thirty-first day of May, in the year one thousand seven hundred and twenty-seven, erecting the said *Royal Bank*, and by the said letters patent, thereafter granted to the said Bank, bearing date the first day of November, in the year one thousand seven hundred and thirty-eight, in as ample manner and form, as if the same were all therein particularly mentioned and repeated.

FOURTH WARRANT.

His Majesty ordained a charter to pass the Seals of Scotland,

confirming the privileges formerly granted to the Bank;

A a And

[186]

FOURTH WARRANT.

And considering, That, if the Corporation of the said *Royal Bank* had power to assign and transfer the aforesaid One hundred and eleven thousand pounds of Equivalent Stock, they would thereby be enabled to carry on the business of Banking to a greater extent, which would be of great advantage to that part of the united kingdom, and would very much promote the trade, manufactures, and improvements of that country, his Majesty thereby gave and granted full power and authority to the Governor, Deputy-Governor, and Directors of the said Company of *The Royal Bank of Scotland*, by and with the direction and approbation of a General Court of the Proprietors thereof, to assign and transfer the said sum of One hundred and eleven thousand pounds of Equivalent Stock, originally subscribed into the said *Royal Bank*, or such part of it as they should find necessary,

and further impowering the Governor, &c. with the approbation of a General Court of Proprietors, to transfer the said 111,000l. of Equivalent Stock.

to

to any perfon or perfons, bodies politic and corporate, notwithftanding that the fame is incorporated of the Stock of the faid *Royal Bank;* and his Majefty thereby declared, That fuch tranffers or affignments fhould be good, valid, and fufficient to fuch perfon or perfons, bodies politic and corporate, who fhould purchafe the faid Equivalent Stock, or any part thereof. And to remove any doubt as to the fubfifting of the faid Corporation or Company of *The Royal Bank of Scotland,* after the transferring the faid Equivalent Stock, his Majefty thereby declared and directed, that, notwithftanding of fuch transfers or affignments of the faid Equivalent Stock, the faid Corporation or Company of *The Royal Bank of Scotland* fhould and might, after fuch transfers or affignments, as aforefaid, continue for ever, and have perpetual fucceffion, and enjoy all the privileges, benefits, and advantages whatfoever,

FOURTH WARRANT.

Such transfers to be good and effectual to the purchafers.

The Corporation of the Bank to fubfift notwithftanding of fuch transfers,

and continue to enjoy all the privileges formerly granted to them.

[188]

FOURTH WARRANT.

whatsoever, given and granted to them by the said two recited charters or letters patent, as if no such transfers or assignments had been made; and from and after the making of such transfers or assignments of the said Equivalent Stock, the monies arising therefrom should be and be deemed part of the Stock of the said Company or Corporation of *The Royal Bank*, and should belong to the Proprietors of the said Bank, in proportion to their shares and interest; and should be assignable or transferable in such and the like manner, *mutatis mutandis*, as the shares in the Capital Stock and yearly Fund are now assignable or might be assigned; and that upon such assigning or transferring of the said sum of One hundred and eleven thousand pounds of Equivalent Stock, or any part thereof, the Proprietors of the said Stock in the said *Royal Bank*, or the majority of them, in a General Court, should and might

The money arising from the sale of such Equivalent Stock, should be deemed part of the Stock of the Bank,

transferable in the same manner as the shares in the Capital Stock and yearly fund are new assignable.

The Proprietors might authorise the Court of Directors to receive the monies arising from the sales of said Equivalent Stock.

might, and they are thereby impowered and authorised to give sufficient authority to their Court of Directors, or such other person or persons as they should please to nominate and appoint, to receive the money that should be paid or payable to the Company or Corporation, upon such transfers or assignments of the said Equivalent Stock; and also that it should and might be lawful to and for the majority of the Proprietors of the said Company and Corporation, present at their General Court or Courts, and they are thereby impowered and authorised to impower their said Court of Directors, from time to time, to lay out and invest the money that should be received for the said Equivalent Stock, or any part thereof, upon such security and securities as the said majority of the said Proprietors in such General Courts should think fit to direct and appoint; and that the interest and produce arising

FOURTH WARRANT.

The Proprietors might authorise the Court of Directors to lay out such monies upon such securities as they should think fit.

FOURTH WARRANT. The intereſt and produce ariſing from ſuch monies to be divided amongſt the Proprietors, as a General Court ſhould direct.	ſing by and from ſuch money, or the ſecurities taken for the ſame, ſhould be divided to and amongſt the Proprietors of the Stock of *The Royal Bank*, in ſuch way and manner, and by ſuch methods, as the General Court of the ſaid Company and Corporation, or the majority of them, ſhould direct and determine; and that the ſaid money ſo
The ſaid money, and ſecurities taken for the ſame, to be ſubject to the ſame rules and directions as the preſent Capital Stock of the Company.	paid in, and the ſecurities taken for the ſame, ſhould be under the direction of the General Courts of the Corporation, and the Governor, Deputy-Governor, and Directors of the ſaid Company or Corporation, in the ſame way and manner, and ſubject to the ſame rules and directions as the preſent Capital Stock of the ſaid Corporation or Company are now under; to the end that a ſure and permanent fund might ſubſiſt for the credit of the ſaid Bank, and ſecurity of ſuch as dealt with them. Provided always, That no dividend ſhould be made to the Proprietors

Proprietors of the said Stock of the said Company, after such assignments or transfers of the said Stock, but out of the interest of the money arising from the sale or sales of the said Equivalent Stock, and out of the profit arising and to arise, by borrowing and lending of money, and dealing in the trade and business of Banking, as aforesaid. And his Majesty did, for himself, his heirs, and successors, grant and declare, That these his letters patent should be in and by all things valid and effectual in the law, according to the true intent and meaning of the same, and should be taken, construed, and adjudged, in the most favourable and beneficial sense, for the best advantage of the said Corporation, notwithstanding of any misrecital, defaults, uncertainty, or imperfection, in these his Majesty's letters patent, as by the said grant or letters patent, passed under the Seal appointed

FOURTH WARRANT.

Dividends shall only be made out of the interest of the said monies, and from the profits arising from Banking.

These presents to be construed in the most favourable sense for the advantage of the Corporation.

FOURTH WARRANT.

ed by the Treaty of Union to be kept in Scotland, in place of the Great Seal thereof, relation being thereunto had, doth and may more fully and at large appear. And confidering, That the said Corporation of *The Royal Bank of Scotland* have, by their moft humble application to his Majefty, reprefenting, That, fince obtaining thefe patents, *The Royal Bank* have carried on the bufinefs of Banking in Scotland much to the benefit of the trade, manufactures, and improvements of that part of the united kingdom, and that they, agreeable to the powers vefted in them, by the letters patent of his late glorious Majefty King George the Second, dated tenth November one thoufand feven hundred and thirty-eight, before recited, had lately, from their calls and profits, added to their Capital Stock the fum of Thirty-eight thoufand fix hundred and fifty-two pounds one penny and feven-twelfths of

Recital of the petition of *The Royal Bank* to his Majefty,

That they have carried on the bufinefs of Banking to the benefit of trade, &c.:

of a penny Sterling, and whereby the same now amounts to One hundred and fifty thousand pounds Sterling; and that they would be able to carry the good purposes of their erection on to a higher degree, and with greater benefit to the country, if they were impowered to enlarge their present Capital to the extent of One hundred and fifty thousand pounds Sterling more, in the same way or manner, and with such provisions as are contained in the said charter, dated first November one thousand seven hundred and thirty-eight: And therefore praying, That his Majesty would be most graciously pleased, by letters patent under the Great Seal of Scotland, to ratify and confirm their privileges, authorities, and rights formerly granted to them, by the foresaid charter erecting *The Royal Bank*, and the said other several before recited letters patent obtained by them; and to autho-

FOURTH WARRANT.

That it would be highly advantageous to the country were they allowed to enlarge their capital to the extent of 150,000 l. more.

Praying his Majesty to confirm their privileges;

FOURTH
WARRANT.

and to impower the Governor, &c. with approbation of a General Court of Proprietors, to enlarge their capital by a fum not exceeding 150,000l. by fubfcriptions of Equivalent Stock, land fecurity, &c.

rife and impower the Governor, Deputy-Governor, and Directors of the faid *Royal Bank of Scotland*, with the direction and approbation of a General Court of Proprietors, to enlarge their prefent Capital to any fum not exceeding One hundred and fifty thoufand pounds Sterling, fo as the Stock may amount in all to Three hundred thoufand pounds Sterling; and to make fuch enlargement by taking in fubfcriptions of Equivalent Stock, by heritable land fecurities, or by any other way that the Directors of *The Royal Bank*, by and with confent of the faid General Court of Proprietors, fhould judge fafe and beneficial to the Bank, in the fame way and manner, and with fuch powers and provifions as are contained in the faid charter and letters patent, dated firft November one thoufand feven hundred and thirty-eight. And confidering fuch petition has been referred to the Lord Advocate

vocate of Scotland for his opinion, what might be reasonable and fitting for his Majesty to do therein; and his Majesty having taken into his royal consideration the said petition, and the report thereupon made by the Lord Advocate of Scotland, and being willing to give all proper encouragement to such an undertaking; therefore his Majesty, in compliance with the said request, and by virtue of his prerogative royal, and of his especial grace, certain knowledge, and mere motion, ordains a charter to be made and passed under the Seal appointed by the Treaty of Union to be kept in Scotland, in place of the Great Seal thereof, ratifying and confirming, as his Majesty does hereby ratify and confirm, all the privileges, authorities, and rights formerly granted to the said Company or Corporation of *The Royal Bank of Scotland*, by the said charter or letters patent, bearing date the thirty-

FOURTH WARRANT.

The petition referred to the Lord Advocate of Scotland;

and the same, with the Lord Advocate's report thereon, being taken into consideration,

his Majesty ordained a charter to pass the Seals of Scotland,

confirming the privileges formerly granted to the Bank;

FOURTH
WARRANT.

thirty-firſt day of May in the year one thouſand ſeven hundred and twenty-ſeven, erecting the ſaid *Royal Bank;* and by the ſaid letters patent thereafter granted to the ſaid *Bank,* bearing date the firſt day of November, in the year one thouſand ſeven hundred and thirty-eight; and by the ſaid charter and letters patent, dated ſixteenth May one thouſand ſeven hundred and ſeventy, in as ample manner and form, as if the ſame were all herein particularly mentioned and repeated: And to the end that the ſaid *Royal Bank of Scotland* may be the better encouraged to proceed in ſo laudable an undertaking of Banking, and ſo much for the benefit of the ſubjects of that part of the united kingdom; and conſidering, That the preſent Capital of the ſaid Company of *The Royal Bank of Scotland* is not ſufficient to anſwer the ſeveral good purpoſes of their erection, and that the

the addition of a sum to their present Capital may facilitate their operations, and enable them to be further useful to that part of the united kingdom, by carrying on their business of Banking to a greater extent, and with more security, which would be of great advantage to and much promote the trade, manufactures, and improvements of that country; therefore his Majesty hereby gives full power and authority to the Governor, Deputy-Governor, and Directors of the said Company of *The Royal Bank of Scotland*, by and with the direction and approbation of a General Court of the Proprietors thereof, to enlarge their present Capital of One hundred and fifty thousand pounds Sterling, to any sum not exceeding Three hundred thousand pounds Sterling in the whole; and that either by taking subscriptions of other Equivalent Stock, not already subscribed into the said Bank, or by

FOURTH WARRANT.

and authorising the Governor, Deputy-Governor, & Directors of the said Company, with approbation of a General Court of Proprietors, to enlarge their capital to any sum not exceeding 300,000l.

FOURTH WARRANT.

by taking in fubfcriptions of certain fums of money upon land fecurity, or any other ways and means that the faid Directors of *The Royal Bank of Scotland*, by the confent of the faid General Court of the Proprietors, fhall judge moft fafe and beneficial to the Corporation of the faid *Royal Bank*; and to that end, his Majefty does, by thefe prefents, authorife and impower the faid Directors to take and receive fuch fubfcriptions, in fuch way and manner as the General Court of the faid Proprietors fhall direct: And for completing the faid additional ftock of One hundred and fifty thoufand pounds Sterling, it fhall and may be lawful to and for the Proprietors of the faid Company of *The Royal Bank*, or the majority of them, in any General Court of the faid Company, to be held as in the faid former charter is mentioned and directed, either to allow the Proprietors of fuch part

The Directors to receive fubfcriptions in fuch way as the General Court of Proprietors fhall direct,

for completing the additional ftock of 150,000l.

of

of the Equivalent Stock, to subscribe such further or other part of the stock of the said Company into the stock of the said Company of *The Royal Bank*, not exceeding in the whole the sum of One hundred and fifty thousand pounds, upon such terms and conditions, and at such times as the majority of the Proprietors of *The Royal Bank of Scotland* in such General Courts shall limit and appoint; or it shall and may be lawful for the majority of the Proprietors of the said *Royal Bank of Scotland* to take in such additional stock of One hundred and fifty thousand pounds Sterling, by a voluntary subscription, either of money upon heritable security or otherwise, and upon such terms and conditions, and at such times, as the majority of the Proprietors of the said Company of *The Royal Bank of Scotland*, in such General Court, shall limit, direct, and appoint. And his Majesty

FOURTH WARRANT.

To allow the Proprietors of Equivalent Stock to subscribe such part of the Stock of the said Company into the Stock of *The Royal Bank*, not exceeding 150,000 l.;

or to take such additional stock by a voluntary subscription, either of money, heritable security, or otherwise.

FOURTH WARRANT.

The stock so subscribed, &c. to be under the direction of the Corporation of The Royal Bank, as the stock formerly subscribed.

jesty doth hereby declare and direct, That such stock of *The Equivalent Company*, so to be subscribed in the terms aforesaid, and such subscriptions so to be made in money upon heritable security or otherwise, shall, from and after such subscription, be under the management, care, and direction of the Corporation or Company of *The Royal Bank*, from the time of such subscription, in the same way and manner as the stock formerly subscribed was, by the said former charters or letters patent, directed and appointed; and that the same, and the Proprietors, subscribers thereof, shall and

To have the same privileges as the Proprietors of the first subscribed stock.

may, upon the terms and conditions so to be limited and appointed, from the time of such subscription as aforesaid, have all the same privileges and liberties as the Proprietors of the first subscribed stock, and proportions thereof, shall have and enjoy; and that such new stock, so to be subscribed,

bed, shall be transferable in the same way and manner, and upon the same terms and conditions, as the present stock of the said Company is now transferable, by virtue of or under the said charter of the thirty-firſt day of May, in the year one thouſand ſeven hundred and twenty-ſeven; and charter dated the firſt of November one thouſand ſeven hundred and thirty-eight; and charter dated the ſixteenth May one thouſand ſeven hundred and ſeventy; and the Proprietors of ſuch ſubſcribed ſtock ſhall be entitled to have and receive the ſame, or the like dividends, as ſhall from time to time be declared upon the preſent Capital of the ſaid Corporation or Company. And his Majeſty, for the better encouragement of the ſaid *Royal Bank* to proceed in and continue their undertaking of Banking, ſo much for the benefit of the ſubjects of that part of our united kingdom, declares and directs,

FOURTH WARRANT.

Transferable in the ſame way therewith.

FOURTH WARRANT.

Notwithstanding the Parliament should redeem the Equivalent Stock, the Corporation of *The Royal Bank* shall still continue;

rects, That, in case the Parliament of Great Britain shall, at any time or times, think proper to redeem the said Equivalent Stock, or such part thereof as has been or shall be subscribed into the said Company of *The Royal Bank of Scotland*, or that the said Corporation or Company of *The Royal Bank of Scotland* shall assign or transfer the same as aforesaid, yet, that the said Corporation or Company of *The Royal Bank of Scotland*, notwithstanding thereof, shall and may, after such redemption or transfer, as aforesaid, continue for ever, and have perpetual

and enjoy all former privileges, except the share in the annual fund of 10,000l.

succession, and enjoy all the privileges, benefits, and advantages whatsoever, given and granted to them by the said recited charters or letters patent, except the share or interest in the said annual fund of Ten thousand pounds, as aforesaid, as if no such redemption or transfer were had or made; and from and after such redemption or

transfer

[203]

transfer, all perfons having any fhare or intereft, or ftock paid into or gained by the faid Company, to carry on the trade of the faid Company, fhall be and be deemed Members of the faid Company, and be entitled to all the benefits, privileges, and advantages thereof, in proportion to their refpective fhares and interefts in the faid money or ftock as aforefaid; and the faid money or ftock fo paid, or to be paid, fhall be affignable or tranfferable in fuch and the like manner, *mutatis mutandis*, as the faid fhares in the Capital Stock and yearly Fund are now affignable or may be affigned; and that, upon fuch redemption or transfer as aforefaid, the Proprietors of the faid ftock in the faid *Royal Bank*, or the majority of them in a General Court, fhall and may, and they are hereby impowered and authorifed to give fufficient authority to their Court of Directors, or fuch other perfon or perfons

FOURTH WARRANT.

After redemption, all perfons having intereft or ftock paid into or gained by the Company, to carry on the trade of the Company, fhall be deemed Members, and entitled to all advantages thereof;

and the ftock fo paid, or to be paid, fhall be transferable, in like manner as the fhares in the Capital Stock and yearly fund were then affignable.

The Proprietors in a General Court, or majority of them, impowered to give fufficient authority to their Court of Directors, or fuch perfons as they fhall nominate, to receive the money payable to the Company upon fuch redemption as aforefaid, and difcharge the fame.

FOURTH
WARRANT.

persons as they shall please to nominate and appoint, to receive the money that should be paid or payable to the Company or Corporation, upon such redemption or transfer as aforesaid, and give receipts, acquittances, or discharges for the same; and also, That it shall and may be lawful to and for

The Proprietors may authorise the Court of Directors to lay out such monies upon such securities as they should think fit.

the majority of the said Proprietors of the said Company and Corporation present at their General Court or Courts, and they are hereby impowered and authorised to impower their said Court of Directors, from time to time, to lay out and invest the money that shall, upon such redemption or transfer, be paid as aforesaid, upon such security and securities as the said majority of the Proprietors in such General Court shall think fit to direct and appoint;

The interest and produce arising from such monies to be divided amongst the Proprietors, as a General Court shall direct.

and that the interest and produce arising by and from such money, or the securities taken for the same, shall be divided to and amongst the Proprietors

FOURTH WARRANT.

tors of the Stock of *The Royal Bank*, in such way and manner, and by such methods, as the General Court of the said Company or Corporation, or the majority of them, shall direct and determine; and that the said money so paid in, and the securities taken for the same, shall be under the direction of the General Courts of the Corporation, and the Governor, Deputy-Governor, and Directors of the said Company or Corporation, in the same way and manner, and subject to the same directions and authorities as the present Capital Stock of the said Corporation or Company are now under; to the end that a sure and permanent fund may subsist for the credit of the said Bank, and security of such as deal with them. Provided always, That no dividend shall be made to the Proprietors of the said Stock of the said Company, after such redemption or transfer as aforesaid, but out of the interest

The said money, and securities taken for the same, to be subject to the same rules and directions as the present Capital Stock of the Company.

Dividends shall only be made out of the interest of the said monies, and from the profits arising from Banking.

FOURTH
WARRANT.

interest of money payable to them, upon such redemption or transfer as aforesaid, and out of the profit arising and to arise by borrowing and lending of money, and dealing in the trade and business of Banking, as aforesaid. And his Majesty doth, for himself, his heirs, and successors, grant and declare, That these his letters patent shall be in and by all things valid and effectual in the law, according to the true intent and meaning of the same, and shall be taken, construed, and adjudged, in the most favourable and beneficial sense, for the best advantage of the said Corporation, notwithstanding of any misrecital, defaults, uncertainty, or imperfection, in these his Majesty's letters patent. And his Majesty doth hereby, for himself, his heirs, and successors, covenant, grant, and agree to and with the said Corporation or Body Politic, and their successors, That he, his

These presents to be construed in the most favourable sense for the advantage of the Corporation.

His Majesty covenants to give such further privileges as he may lawfully grant;

his heirs, and succeffors, fhall and will, from time to time, and at all times hereafter, upon the humble fuit and requeft of the faid Corporation or Body Politic, and their fucceffors, give and grant unto them all fuch further and other privileges, authorities, matters, and things, for rendering more effectual this his grant, according to the true intent and meaning of thefe prefents, which he or they can and may lawfully grant, and as fhall be reafonably advifed and devifed by the counfel learned of the faid Corporation or Body Politic for the time being, and fhall be approved of by the Lord Advocate or Solicitor General in Scotland of his Majefty, his heirs, and fucceffors, on his or their behalf. And his Majefty doth further will and command, That this Charter do pafs the Great Seal *per faltum*, without paffing any other feal or regifter. For doing whereof, this fhall be, as well to the

FOURTH WARRANT.

which fhall be devifed by their own counfel, and approved of by the Lord Advocate or Solicitor General for Scotland for the time.

FOURTH WARRANT.

the Director of our Chancery for writing the same, as to the Keeper of the said Seal for causing the said Seal to be appended thereto, a sufficient war-warrant.—Given at our Court at St James's this tenth day of June one thousand seven hundred and eighty-three, in the twenty-third year of our reign.

FIFTH

WARRANT

OF

THE CHARTER

CONFIRMING AND GRANTING

NEW PRIVILEGES

TO THE

Royal Bank of Scotland.

O U R *SOVEREIGN LORD* confidering, Preamble. That, by an Act of Parliament made and paffed in the fifth year of the reign of his Majefty King George the Firft, entitled, *An Act for settling certain yearly funds, payable out of the Revenues of* Scotland, *to satisfy the public Debts in* Scotland, *and other uses mentioned in the Treaty of Union; and to discharge the Equivalents claimed on behalf of* Scotland,

FIFTH
WARRANT.  Scotland, *in terms of the said Treaty; and for obviating all future disputes, charges, and expences concerning these Equivalents*; it is enacted,

Reciting the act of Parliament 1719, concerning the L.10,000 Annuity payable to the Creditors of the Public in Scotland.

amongst other things, That yearly, and every year, from the Feast of the Nativity of St John the Baptist, one thousand seven hundred and nineteen years, the full sum of Ten thousand pounds of lawful money of Great Britain shall be a yearly Fund for the particular purposes in that act expressed concerning the same, and shall continue and be payable in the manner therein particularly expressed for ever, subject nevertheless to redemption by Parliament, according to a *proviso* in the said act contained in that behalf. And it is thereby further enacted,

His Majesty authorised to incorporate the Proprietors of the debts stated to amount to L.248,550 : 0 : 9½,

That it should and might be lawful to and for his Majesty, by letters patent under the Great Seal of Great Britain, to incorporate all and every the Proprietors of the debts and sums of money,

money, stated to amount to the principal sum of Two hundred and thirty thousand three hundred and eight pounds nine shillings ten pence and five sixth parts of a penny, due to the creditors of the public in Scotland, on the twenty-fourth day of June one thousand seven hundred and fourteen years, and Eighteen thousand two hundred and forty-one pounds ten shillings ten pence and two thirds of a penny, stated due to William Paterson, Esq. making together Two hundred and forty-eight thousand five hundred and fifty pounds and nine pence halfpenny, to be one Body Politic and Corporate, by such name as his Majesty should think most proper, and that by such name the said Corporation should have perpetual succession, subject to such redemption as in the said act is appointed; with such powers to do and perform all matters appertaining to them to do and perform,

touching

FIFTH WARRANT.

due to the creditors of the public in Scotland,

by such name as he should think fit.

touching or concerning the said capital sums, and the said yearly fund payable in respect thereof, as his Majesty by the same letters patent should think fit to grant. And it was thereby enacted, That the said capital sum, amounting to Two hundred forty-eight thousand five hundred and fifty pounds and nine pence halfpenny, should be, and be deemed to be, the Capital or Joint Stock of the said Corporation; and that the shares of the Members of and in the same should be from time to time assignable, transferable, and deviseable, in such manner as his Majesty by such letters patent should prescribe and appoint, until the redemption thereof; and that the same should be deemed to be personal or moveable estates, and should go to executors or administrators, and should not be liable to any arrestments or attachments that should be laid thereon. And it is thereby enacted,

That

FIFTH WARRANT.

And the said L.248,550:0:9½, should be the Capital or Joint Stock of the Corporation,

and be deemed personal or moveable estates,

not liable to arrestments or attachments.

That all and every the Members of the said Corporation should have and be entitled to an annuity or yearly sum, in proportion to his or their share in the said capital sum and stock of Two hundred and forty-eight thousand five hundred and fifty pounds and nine pence halfpenny; and the said annuity should be paid in the manner in the said act mentioned, and to and for no other use, intent, or purpose whatsoever. And it was further enacted, That, above the said annuity of Ten thousand pounds per annum, there should be paid to the said Corporation and their successors, until the redemption of such annual sum, the further annual sum of Six hundred pounds per annum, towards the necessary charges of the management thereof, as in and by the said act of Parliament, amongst other clauses and things therein contained, relation being thereunto had, doth more fully and

FIFTH WARRANT.

L. 600 per annum to be paid to the Corporation for charges of management.

[214]

FIFTH WARRANT.

Recital of the charter erecting the Proprietors of the forefaid debt into a Corporation, by the name of the EQUIVALENT COMPANY.

and at large appear. And confidering, That his faid Majefty King George the Firft, of glorious memory, by his letters patent, bearing date at Weftminfter, the twenty-firft day of November, in the eleventh year of his reign, in purfuance of the faid act of Parliament, and by virtue of his prerogative royal, and likewife of his efpecial grace, certain knowledge, and mere motion, did give, grant, make, ordain, declare, appoint, and eftablifh, That all and every perfon or perfons, natives and foreigners, bodies politic and corporate, who then were Proprietors of the debts and fums of money fo ftated to amount to Two hundred and forty-eight thoufand five hundred and fifty pounds and ninepence halfpenny, or who, by any lawful title, derived, or to be derived, from, by, or under the faid Proprietors at any time thereafter, fhould have, and be entitled to any part, fhare, or intereft therein;

fhould

should be, and be called, one Body Politic and Corporate of themselves, in deed and name, by the name of the EQUIVALENT COMPANY; and that such Corporation, and their successors, should have perpetual succession, subject to such redemption as is therein mentioned, and should and might have and use a common seal, and should, by that name, be capable to sue and be sued; and that the sum of Two hundred forty-eight thousand five hundred and fifty pounds and nine pence halfpenny, should be accepted, deemed, and esteemed the Capital or Joint Stock of the said Corporation, and all the Proprietors of such stock should be Members of the said Corporation; and that the said annuity of Ten thousand pounds per annum should be paid to the said Company or their Cashier, to be divided and distributed to and amongst the several Proprietors, in proportion to their respective

FIFTH WARRANT.

The foresaid L.248,550 : 0 : 9¼ to be the Capital or Joint Stock of the EQUIVALENT COMPANY:

And the annuity of L.10,000, payable to the Company or their Cashier, to be divided amongst the Proprietors, according to their shares in the stock.

FIFTH
WARRANT.

spective shares in the said Capital or Joint Stock. And that his said Majesty did thereby further order and direct,

The stock of the Company to be transferable.

limit, and appoint, That the said stock should be transferable and assignable; and all assignments or transfers of the said capital stock, or yearly fund, or any part thereof, should be in the manner, and according to the methods thereby directed: And likewise ap-

The L.600 is payable to the EQUIVALENT COMPANY, or any person to be appointed by them, under their seal, to receive the same.

pointed, That the said annual sum of Six hundred pounds for charges of management, should be paid to the said Corporation, or such as they should authorise, under their common seal, to receive the same, for the uses of the said Corporation, as by the said grant or letters patent, passed under the Great Seal of Great Britain, relation being thereunto had, doth and may

Recital of the Charter granting the power of Banking, &c. in Scotland, upon petition of the EQUIVALENT COMPANY,

more fully and at large appear. And whereas by charter or letters patent, passed under the Seal appointed by the Treaty of Union to be kept in Scotland,

FIFTH WARRANT.

Scotland, in place of the Great Seal thereof, and bearing date the thirty-first day of May one thousand seven hundred and twenty-seven, reciting to the effect before recited, and also reciting that the said Corporation of the *Equivalent Company*, by their most humble application to his said late Majesty, requested, That he would be graciously pleased, by letters patent under the Great Seal of Scotland, to enable such of the Proprietors of the said Corporation as should subscribe their stock for that purpose, to have the power of Banking in Scotland only, with liberty to borrow and lend upon security there; that the said Corporation might be for that purpose impowered to take subscriptions at Edinburgh from their Members, for such share of the stock as they should incline to subject to such Trade or Banking, under such regulations as they by bye-laws should appoint; and that such subscri-

to such of the Members as should subscribe their stock for that purpose.

E e   bed

[218]

FIFTH WARRANT.

Such subscribed stock only to be subject to the transactions of Banking, & thereafter to be transferable from the other stock of the EQUIVALENT COMPANY, and at Edinburgh only.

bed stock only should be affected by the transactions relating to Banking, and (after being so subscribed) become transferable from the other stock of the Company, and at Edinburgh only; and would erect such subscribers into a Corporation for that purpose; and that such power of Banking, so established, would manifestly tend to the great benefit and advantage of that part of the kingdom; his Majesty, being willing to give all proper encouragement to such an undertaking, therefore his said Majesty, in compliance with the said request, and by virtue of his prerogative royal, and of his Majesty's especial grace, certain knowledge, and mere motion, and for the benefit of his subjects in that part of

A Charter ordained to pass the Seals of Scotland,

the united kingdom, ordained a charter to be made and passed under the Seal appointed by the Treaty of Union to be kept in Scotland, in place of the Great Seal thereof, nominating, authorising,

[219]

authorifing, and appointing, as his Majefty thereby nominated, authorifed, and appointed the perfons therein named, or any three of them, in fuch way and manner as they, or the majority of them, fhould direct, to take and receive at Edinburgh all fuch voluntary fubfcriptions as fhould be made, on or before the twenty-ninth day of September one thoufand feven hundred and twenty-feven years, by any perfon or perfons, Members or Proprietors of the faid *Equivalent Company*, who had, or fhould have credit for ftock in the books of the faid Company at Edinburgh, at the time of fuch fubfcription, of all or any of fuch part or fhare of the ftock of the faid *Equivalent Company*, as he, fhe, or they, fhould think proper, for and towards raifing a fund for the more effectually carrying on the faid trade and bufinefs of Banking there, and the ufes therein after mentioned; which faid fubfcription

FIFTH WARRANT.

authorifing the Directors of the faid EQUIVALENT COMPANY, or any three of them, in fuch way as the majority of them fhall direct, to receive at Edinburgh all fuch voluntary fubfcriptions as fhould be made on or before the 29th day of September 1727, by the Proprietors of the faid Company.

FIFTH
WARRANT.

Which subscriptions are to be entered in books to be kept for that purpose.

The stock so subscribed, to be under the management of the Corporation thereby established.

tion the said Proprietors were thereby impowered to make, and the same should be fairly entered in books to be kept for that purpose; and the then present stock of the said *Equivalent Company*, so to be subscribed as aforesaid, should, from and after the time of such subscription, be under the order, management, and direction of the Company thereby established. And his Majesty, by virtue of the said prerogative, and likewise of his especial grace, certain knowledge, and mere motion, gave, granted, made, ordained, constituted, declared, appointed, and established, That all and every person and persons, natives and foreigners, bodies politic and corporate, Proprietors of the said stock, who should subscribe any share or shares of the said stock, and who, as executors, administrators, successors, or assignees, or by any other lawful title, to be derived from, by, or under the said subscribers,

bers, at any time or times thereafter, should have or be entitled to any part, share, or interest of or in the said stock so to be subscribed as aforesaid, should be and be called one Body Politic and Corporate of themselves, in deed and name, by the name of *The Royal Bank of Scotland*; and that such Corporation, and their successors, by the said name, should have perpetual succession, and should and might have and use a common seal, and they and their successors, by the same name, should be able and capable in law, to sue and implead, pursue and defend, answer and be answered, in all or any of his Majesty's Courts within Scotland; and that they and their successors, by the name aforesaid, should and might be able and capable in law, to have, purchase, receive, possess, enjoy, and retain to them and their successors, lands, rents, tenements, and hereditaments, of what kind, nature, or quality

FIFTH WARRANT.

The subscribers to be called by the name of *The Royal Bank of Scotland*, and by that name to have perpetual succession, and a common Seal, be capable in law to sue and be sued, in any of the Courts within Scotland.

To purchase lands, &c. in Scotland, and to sell the same.

FIFTH WARRANT.

The Royal Bank to have the power of Banking within Scotland.

To lend any fum at any intereft not exceeding lawful intereft, upon perfonal and real fecurity, and pledges of any kind.

The Royal Bank may keep the cafh of other perfons, and borrow, owe, and take up mo-

quality foever, in Scotland only; and alfo to fell, grant, demife, analzie, or difpone the fame: And his Majefty did thereby, for himfelf, his heirs, and fucceffors, grant unto the faid Company of *The Royal Bank of Scotland*, and their fucceffors for ever, full power and liberty to exercife the rights and powers of Banking, in that part of the united kingdom called Scotland only; and in particular to lend to any perfon or perfons, bodies politic or corporate, fuch fum and fums of money, as they fhould think fit, at any intereft not exceeding lawful intereft, on real or perfonal fecurity; and particularly on pledges of any kind whatfoever, of any goods, wares, merchandifes, or other effects whatfoever, in fuch way and manner as to the faid Company fhould feem proper and convenient; and that the faid Company might keep the money or cafh of any perfon or perfons, bodies politic and corporate

corporate whatsoever, and might borrow, owe, or take up in Scotland, on their bills or notes payable on demand, to be signed in such manner, and by such persons, as the Court of Directors therein after mentioned should direct and appoint, or in such other manner as the said Court of Directors should think fit, any sum or sums of money whatsoever. And his Majesty did thereby declare, direct, and appoint, That the said Company should not, at any time or times, deal or trade, or permit or suffer any person or persons whatsoever, either in trust or for the benefit of the same, to deal or trade with any of the stock, money, or effects, of or any ways belonging to the said Corporation, in the buying or selling of any goods, wares, or merchandises whatsoever; provided, that nothing therein contained should any ways be construed to extend to hinder the said Corporation from dealing in bills

FIFTH WARRANT.

ney on their bills or notes payable on demand.

A prohibition to trade with the money or stock of the Company, in buying or selling wares of any sort.

Allowance nevertheless to deal in bills of exchange, in buying bullion, &c.

FIFTH WARRANT.

and selling wares *bona fide* pledged,

and lands, &c. purchased, and the produce thereof.

bills of exchange, or in buying or selling bullion, gold, or silver in Scotland only, or extend to hinder the said Corporation from selling any goods, wares, merchandises, or effects whatsoever, which should really and *bona fide* be pledged, left, or deposited with the said Corporation, for money lent and advanced thereon, and which should not be redeemed at the time agreed on, or from selling such lands, rents, tenements, or hereditaments, as they should purchase, in virtue of the powers thereby given, or from selling such goods as should or might be the produce of lands purchased by the said Corporation. And for the better accomplishment of the ends and intentions proposed by the erecting of the said Corporation, and for making and establishing a continual succession of fit persons to be Managers and Directors of the said Corporation, it was thereby ordained and appointed, That there should

should be, from time to time, a Governor, Deputy-Governor, nine Ordinary Directors, and nine Extraordinary Directors, to be chosen out of the Members of the said Company; who were to have such qualifications, and to be chosen annually, in the manner and according to the rules and directions therein mentioned; and that five or more should be called *A Court of Directors*, for ordering, managing, and directing all affairs of the said Corporation, in manner above mentioned; and no Governor, Deputy-Governor, or Director, or any officer nominated by them, should be capable to sit, vote, or act, or to exercise, use, or discharge any such office, until he had first taken and subscribed the several oaths which then were, or, by any subsequent law, should be directed to be taken by all persons bearing or holding any office, civil or military, under his Majesty, his heirs, and successors.

FIFTH WARRANT.

That there shall be, from time to time, a Governor, Deputy-Governor, nine Ordinary, & nine Extraordinary Directors, for managing the affairs of the Corporation. The Governor, Deputy-Governor, and nine Ordinary Directors, or any five of them, to be called *A Court of Directors*.

No Governor, Deputy-Governor, or Director, nor any officer or servant under them, shall be capable to act, until they have taken the oaths to the Government.

[226]

FIFTH WARRANT.

The Court of Directors may call General Courts of Proprietors, as prescribed; or, in their default, any nine of the Proprietors;

cessors. And it is thereby further directed, That the said Governor, Deputy-Governor, and Court of Directors, or, in their default, any nine of the Proprietors of the shares of Stock therein specified, should have power and liberty, from time to time, to call General Courts of all the Proprietors, upon giving such notice as therein is prescribed, and there to dispatch any business relating to the government or affairs of the said Corporation, and to

and remove or displace the Governor, Deputy-Governor, & any of the Directors, for misdemeanours, & chuse new ones;

remove or displace the said Governor, Deputy-Governor, and any of the Directors, for any misdemeanours or abuse of their office, and elect and chuse new ones in their room, in manner therein mentioned; and to make bye-laws, constitutions, orders, rules, for managing the business of the said Corporation: And that such Court of

and appoint a Secretary, and other officers, and displace them as they see cause;

Directors might appoint a Secretary and all other officers, and displace them as they should see cause. And, for the better

better carrying on the affairs of the said Corporation, the said Court of Directors, or any nine of them, were directed to inspect, state, and audite the accounts of the Company, and sign and approve thereof, in manner therein directed; and power was thereby given to the General Courts of the said Company, from time to time, by majority of votes, to make such calls upon all and every the Proprietors of the said Stock and Corporation, as to the majority of such General Court should seem proper, so as such calls so to be made did not in the whole exceed fifty pounds upon every hundred pounds of the Subscribed Capital of the said Stock, and so as not above ten pounds in the hundred pounds of the said Subscribed Capital of the said Stock be called at one time; and that such calls should be paid in by the Proprietors, within the time or times so limited by such General Court; and that no person

FIFTH WARRANT.

and inspect, state, and audite the accounts of the Company.

The General Courts may make calls upon the Proprietors;

which are not to exceed 50l. upon the 100l. Capital, and no call to be above 10l. per cent. at a time.

[228]

FIFTH WARRANT.

Any person neglecting to pay such calls shall not be allowed to transfer their Stock, nor receive any dividends or profits till such calls be paid.

person who should refuse or neglect to pay in such calls, should be allowed to transfer or part with any share they respectively had in the said Stock, nor receive any dividends or profits on account thereof, till such calls should by them respectively be paid. And for ascertaining and limiting in what manner, and under what rules the said Capital Stock should and might be assigned and transferred, it was thereby further directed, That there should be forthwith provided and constantly kept in the public office of the said Corpora-

Books for transfers to be kept at Edinburgh.

tion at Edinburgh, a book or books, wherein all assignments or transfers should be entered, and the said stock should be transferable and transferred, according to the methods and forms therein particularly prescribed and set down; and that any person having

Any share of the Stock may be disposed of by last will & testament.

any share or interest in the said Stock might dispose and devise the same by his or her last will and testament; and

[229]

and that all such shares or interests in such Stock should be deemed personal estates, and not be liable to any arrestment or attachment. And it was further declared, That the Cashier of the said Corporation, or any other person by them lawfully authorised, should, from time to time, receive from the said *Equivalent Company*, or any person by them lawfully authorised, their share and proportion of the said annual sum of Ten thousand pounds payable by virtue of the said recited act of parliament, and dividends, in respect of such of the said Stock of the said *Equivalent Company*, so to be subscribed; and that the General Court of the said Company should, at two terms in the year, declare such dividends as they should think proper to be paid to the respective Proprietors. Provided no dividend should be made but out of the share and interest of the yearly annuity of Ten thousand pounds, and

out

FIFTH WARRANT.

The Stock not liable to any arrestment or attachment.

The Cashier of the Corporation, or any other person authorised to receive their proportion of the 10,000 l. annuity.

The General Court, at two times in every year, is to declare a dividend.

No dividend to be made, but out of their share of the 10,000 l. annuity, and the profits of Banking.

FIFTH
WARRANT.

out of the profit arising by borrowing and lending of money, and dealing in the trade and business of Banking; and that such General Court, from time to time, as they should see proper, might repay all or any part of the said sum of fifty pounds per cent. that should at any time have been called by them upon the Stock of the said Company, as by the said grant or letters patent, passed under the Seal appointed by the Treaty of Union to be kept in Scotland, in place of the Great Seal thereof, relation being thereunto had, doth and may more fully and at large appear. And whereas, by charter or letters patent, passed under the Seal appointed by the Treaty of Union to be kept in Scotland, in place of the Great Seal thereof, and bearing date the first day of November in the year one thousand seven hundred and thirty-eight, reciting to the effect before recited, and also reciting, That the

Calls upon the Stock may be repaid.

Recital of the charter anno 1738, confirming and granting new privileges to The Royal Bank.

the said Company or Corporation of *The Royal Bank of Scotland*, by their most humble application to his late Majesty King George II. of glorious memory, representing, That, in pursuance of the foresaid letters patent, certain of the Proprietors of the said *Equivalent Company* did subscribe parts and shares of the said Stock, for the purposes in the said charter or letters patent mentioned, to the extent of One hundred and eleven thousand pounds; and that they had for some years carried on the business of Banking, to the great benefit and advantage of that part of the united kingdom in general, and in particular to merchants carrying on and advancing trade: And further representing, That the annuity to which the Proprietors of the *Equivalent Company*, and in consequence the shares subscribed into *The Royal Bank of Scotland*, being subject to redemption, a doubt might arise,

Whether

FIFTH WARRANT.

That in pursuance of the said letters patent, Proprietors of the *Equivalent Company* did subscribe Stock to the extent of 111,000l.

That the annuity payable to the Proprietors of *Equivalent*, and shares subscribed into *The Royal Bank*, being subject to redemption, a doubt might arise, Whether, upon such redemption, *The Royal Bank* might cease;

FIFTH WARRANT.

and, whether the said sum of 111,000l. must not be divided amongst the Proprietors.

That the then Capital of the Bank was not sufficient to answer the purposes of their erection; and that the addition of a sum not exceeding 40,000l. to the then Capital, making in the whole 151,000l. might facilitate their operations.

Whether, upon the redemption of the capital sum of the said *Equivalent Company* by Parliament, *The Royal Bank of Scotland* might cease and determine; and that it might also be doubted, Whether, in case of redemption, the said sum of One hundred and eleven thousand pounds must not be divided amongst the Proprietors, according to their respective interests in the said Stock at the time of redemption: And further representing, That it was found by experience that the then present Capital of the said Bank was not sufficient to answer the several good ends and purposes of its erection; and that the Proprietors humbly apprehend, that the addition of any sum not exceeding Forty thousand pounds to the then present Capital, making in the whole the sum of One hundred and fifty-one thousand pounds, might facilitate their operations, and enable them to be further useful in that part of of the united kingdom, Whether that addition should be made by subscribing a further sum of Equivalent Stock, heritable land security, or any other way that should appear safe to the said Corporation; and therefore the said Company or Corporation of *The Royal Bank* most humbly requested, That his said late Majesty would be graciously pleased, by letters patent under the Great Seal of Scotland, to ratify and confirm their privileges, authorities, and rights formerly granted, and to remove all doubts concerning the subsisting of the said Corporation, in case of redemption by Parliament; and to authorise and impower the Proprietors of *The Royal Bank* to enlarge their Capital to any sum not exceeding Forty thousand pounds, by taking in subscriptions of Equivalent Stock, by heritable land security, or by any other way that the Directors of *The Royal Bank*, with consent of their General Court

FIFTH WARRANT.

That his Majesty would ratify and confirm their privileges, remove all doubts concerning their subsisting, in case of redemption, and enlarge their Capital, by the addition of a sum not exceeding 40,000l.

[234]

FIFTH WARRANT.

That the Proprietors might be empowered to take and discharge the Public of the aforesaid 111,0ool. and lay out the same as the Directors should judge safe.

Court of Proprietors, should judge safe and beneficial to the Bank: Also, that the Proprietors of the said sum of One hundred and eleven thousand pounds Equivalent Stock might be impowered, by authority of a General Court of Proprietors, to take, acquit, and discharge the Public of the aforesaid sum, and to lay out the same in such way and on such security as the Directors aforesaid should judge safe, to the end that a sure and permanent fund might still subsist for the credit of the Bank, and the safety of such as dealt with them. And his said late Majesty being willing to give all proper encouragement to such an undertaking, therefore his Majesty, in compliance with the said request, and by virtue of his prerogative royal, and of his especial grace, certain knowledge, and mere motion, ordained a charter to be made and passed under the Seal appointed by the Treaty of Union to be kept in Scotland,

The above recital being taken into consideration,

a charter is ordained to pass the Seals of Scotland,

[235]

FIFTH WARRANT.

land, in place of the Great Seal thereof, ratifying and confirming, as his Majesty thereby ratified and confirmed, all the privileges, authorities, and rights, formerly granted to the Company or Corporation of *The Royal Bank of Scotland*, by the said charter or letters patent, bearing date the thirty-first day of May one thousand seven hundred and twenty-seven, as aforesaid, in as ample manner and form, as if the same had been all therein particularly mentioned and repeated. And further, his Majesty thereby gave full power and authority to the Governor, Deputy-Governor, and Directors of the said Company of *The Royal Bank of Scotland*, by and with the direction and approbation of a General Court of the Proprietors, to enlarge their then present Capital to any sum not exceeding Forty thousand pounds, and that either by taking subscriptions of other

confirming all privileges granted to *The Royal Bank*:

and authorising the Governor, Deputy-Governor, & Directors of the said Company, with approbation of a General Court of Proprietors, to enlarge their capital by a sum not exceeding 40,000 l.

FIFTH WARRANT.

The Directors to receive subscriptions in such way as the General Court of Proprietors should direct,

for completing the additional stock of 40,000l.

other Equivalent Stock not then subscribed into the said Bank, or by taking in subscriptions of certain sums of money upon land security, or any other ways and means that the said Directors of *The Royal Bank of Scotland*, by the consent of the said General Court of Proprietors, should judge most safe and beneficial to the Corporation of the said *Royal Bank*; and to that end, his Majesty did thereby authorise and impower the said Directors to take and receive such subscriptions, in such way and manner as the General Court of the said Proprietors should direct: And for completing the said additional Stock of Forty thousand pounds, it should and might be lawful to and for the Proprietors of the said Company of *The Royal Bank*, or the majority of them, in any General Court of the said Company, to be held as in the said former charter is mentioned and directed,

rected, either to allow the Proprietors of such part of the Equivalent Stock, to subscribe such further or other part of the Stock of the said Company into the Stock of the said Company of *The Royal Bank*, not exceeding in the whole the Sum of Forty thousand pounds, upon such terms and conditions, and at such times as the majority of the Proprietors of *The Royal Bank of Scotland*, in such General Courts, should limit and appoint; or it should and might be lawful for the majority of the Proprietors of the said *Royal Bank of Scotland*, to take in such additional Stock of Forty thousand pounds by a voluntary subscription, either of money upon heritable security, or otherways, and upon such terms and conditions, and at such times as the majority of the Proprietors of the said Company of *The Royal Bank of Scotland*, in such General Court, should limit, direct, and appoint.

And

PITT'S WARRANT.

To allow the Proprietors of Equivalent Stock to subscribe such part of the Stock of the said Company into the Stock of *The Royal Bank*, not exceeding 40,000 L.;

or to take such additional stock by a voluntary subscription, either of money, heritable security, or otherwise,

FIFTH
WARRANT.

The stock so subscribed, &c. to be under the direction of the Corporation of *The Royal Bank*, as the stock formerly subscribed.

To have the same privileges as the Proprietors of the first subscribed stock.

And his Majesty did thereby declare and direct, That such Stock of the *Equivalent Company*, so to be subscribed in the terms aforesaid, and such subscriptions so to be made in money upon heritable security, or otherways, should, from and after such subscription, be under the management, care, and direction of the Corporation or Company of *The Royal Bank* from the time of such subscription, in the same way and manner as the Stock formerly subscribed was, by the said former charter or letters patent, directed and appointed; and should and might, upon the terms and conditions so to be limited and appointed, from the time of such subscription, as aforesaid, have all the same privileges and liberties as the Proprietors of the first subscribed Stock should have or enjoy; and that such new Stock, so to be subscribed, should be transferable in the same way and manner, and upon the same

same terms and conditions as the then present Stock of the said Company was transferable, by virtue of or under the said charter of the thirty-first day of May, in the year one thousand seven hundred and twenty-seven; and the Proprietors of such subscribed Stock should be entitled to have and receive the same, or the like dividends, as should, from time to time, be declared upon the then present Capital of the said Corporation or Company. And his said late Majesty, for the better encouragement of the said *Royal Bank* to proceed in and continue their undertaking of Banking, so much for the benefit of the said united kingdom, declared and directed, That, in case the Parliament of Great Britain should, at any time or times, think proper to redeem the said Equivalent Stock, or such part thereof as had been or should be subscribed into the said Company of *The Royal Bank of Scotland*, that the

FIFTH WARRANT.

Transferable in the same way therewith.

Notwithstanding the Parliament should redeem the Equivalent Stock, the Corporation of *The Royal Bank* shall still continue;

FIFTH WARRANT.

and enjoy all former privileges, except the share in the annual fund of 10,000l.

After redemption, all persons having interest or stock paid into or gained by the Company, to carry on the trade of the Company, should be deemed Members, and entitled to all advantages thereof;

the said Corporation or Company of *The Royal Bank of Scotland*, notwithstanding thereof, should and might, after such redemption as aforesaid, continue for ever, and have perpetual succession, and enjoy all the privileges, benefits, and advantages whatsoever, given and granted to them by the said recited charter and letters patent, except the share or interest in the said annual fund of Ten thousand pounds as aforesaid, as if no such redemption were had or made; and from and after such redemption, all persons having any share or interest, or stock paid into or gained by the said Company, to carry on the trade of the said Company, should be and be deemed Members of the said Company, and be entitled to all the benefits, privileges, and advantages thereof, in proportion to their respective shares and interests in the said money or stock as aforesaid; and the said money or stock so paid, or to be be paid, should be assignable or transferable in such and the like manner, *mutatis mutandis*, as the shares in the Capital Stock and yearly Fund were assignable or might be assigned; and that, upon such redemption as aforesaid, the Proprietors of the said stock in the said *Royal Bank*, or the majority of them in a General Court, should and might, and they were thereby impowered and authorised to give sufficient authority to their Court of Directors, or such other person or persons as they should please to nominate and appoint, to receive the money that should be paid or payable to the Company or Corporation, upon such redemption as aforesaid, and give receipts, acquittances, or discharges for the same; and also, That it should and might be lawful to and for the majority of the said Proprietors of the said Company and Corporation present at their General Court or Courts,

H h and

FIFTH WARRANT.

and the stock so paid, or to be paid should be transferable, in like manner as the shares in the Capital Stock and yearly fund were then assignable.

The Proprietors in a General Court, or majority of them, impowered to give sufficient authority to their Court of Directors, or such persons as they should nominate, to receive the money payable to the Company upon such redemption as aforesaid, and discharge the same;

FIFTH WARRANT.

and to impower the Court of Directors, from time to time, to lay out the money that should upon redemption be paid, upon such security as the majority of the Proprietors in such General Court should think fit to appoint.

and they were thereby impowered and authorised to impower their said Court of Directors, from time to time, to lay out and invest the money that should, upon such redemption, be paid as aforesaid, upon such security and securities as the said majority of the Proprietors in such General Court should think fit to direct and appoint;

The interest arising from such money, or securities for the same, to be divided amongst the Proprietors, in such way as the General Court of the said Company should direct.

and the interest and produce arising by and from such money, or the securities taken for the same, should be divided to and amongst the Proprietors of the said stock of *The Royal Bank*, in such way and manner, and by such methods, as the said General Court of the said Company or Corporation, or the majority of them, should direct and determine; and that the said money so paid in, and the securities taken for the same, should be under the direction of the General Courts of the Corporation, and the Governor, Deputy-Governor, and Directors of the said Company

The money so paid, & securities taken for the same, should be under the direction of the General Courts of the Corporation, in the same way as the then Capital Stock;

Company or Corporation, in the same way and manner, and subject to the same directions and authorities as the then present Capital Stock of the said Corporation or Company were under; to the end that a sure and permanent fund might subsist for the credit of the said Bank, and security of such as dealt with them. And his said late Majesty did thereby, for himself, his heirs, and successors, covenant, grant, and agree to and with the said Corporation or Body Politic, and their successors, That he, his heirs, and successors, should and would, from time to time, and at all times thereafter, upon the humble suit and request of the said Corporation or Body Politic, and their successors, give and grant unto them all such further and other privileges, and authorities, matters, and things, for rendering more effectual the said grant, according to the true intent and meaning thereof, which he or they could or might

FIFTH WARRANT.

that a sure fund might subsist for the credit of the Bank, and security of such as dealt with them.

His Majesty to give such further privileges as he might lawfully grant.

FIFTH
WARRANT.

might lawfully grant, and as should be reasonably advised and devised by the counsel learned of the said Corporation or Body Politic, for the time being, and should be approved of by the Lord Advocate or Solicitor General in Scotland, of his Majesty, his heirs, and successors, on his or their behalf, as by the said grant or letters patent, passed under the Seal appointed by the Treaty of Union to be kept in Scotland, in place of the Great Seal thereof, relation being thereunto had, doth and may more fully and at large appear. And whereas, by a charter or letters patent under the Seal appointed by the Treaty of Union to be kept in Scotland, in place of the Great Seal thereof, and bearing date the sixteenth day of May one thousand seven hundred and seventy, reciting to the effect before recited; and also reciting, That the said Company, since obtaining the foresaid charter

Recital of the petition of *The Royal Bank* to his Majesty.

charter erecting *The Royal Bank*, and letters patent afterwards obtained by them, have carried on the business of Banking in Scotland very extensively, and much to the benefit of the trade, manufactures, and improvements, in that part of the united kingdom; but that they, by being debarred of the free use and command of the foresaid capital of one hundred and eleven thousand pounds of Equivalent Stock, are deprived of the power of so effectually forwarding the improvement and trade of the country as they could do, were they enabled to transfer their shares of the said Equivalent Stock, in the same manner as they could have done, legally and effectually, in the character of individual Proprietors, before they were incorporated; and therefore praying, That his Majesty would be graciously pleased, by letters patent under the Great Seal of Scotland, to ratify and confirm their privileges,

PRIVY WARRANT.

That they have carried on the business of Banking to the benefit of trade, &c.:

That it would be highly advantageous to the country were they allowed the free use of said 111,000l. Equivalent Stock, and enabled to transfer the same.

Praying his Majesty to confirm their privileges;

privileges, authorities, and rights, formerly granted by the forefaid charter, erecting *The Royal Bank*, and letters patent afterwards obtained by them; and to authorife and impower the Governor, Deputy-Governor, and Directors of the faid *Royal Bank*, and their fucceffors in office, by authority of a General Court of Proprietors, to transfer their fhares of the Capital Stock of the *Equivalent Company*, or fuch part of it as they fhould find neceffary; and to declare fuch transfers good and fufficient to the receivers; and that the Governor, Deputy-Governor, and Directors of the faid *Royal Bank*, and their fucceffors in office, by authority of a General Court of Proprietors, might be authorifed to lay out the money arifing from the fale or fales, to be made by them of their fhares of the Equivalent Stock, upon lands, bonds, bills, or other good and fufficient fecurity, as fhould appear to be moſt beneficial for the Corporation; therefore his Majeſty ordained a charter to be made and paſſed under the Seal appointed by the Treaty of Union to be kept in Scotland, in place of the Great Seal thereof, ratifying and confirming, as his Majeſty thereby ratified and confirmed all the privileges, authorities, and rights, formerly granted to the ſaid Company or Corporation of *The Royal Bank of Scotland*, by the ſaid charter or letters patent, bearing date the thirty-firſt day of May, in the year one thouſand ſeven hundred and twenty-ſeven, erecting the ſaid *Royal Bank*, and by the ſaid letters patent, thereafter granted to the ſaid Bank, bearing date the firſt day of November, in the year one thouſand ſeven hundred and thirty-eight, in as ample manner and form, as if the ſame were all therein particularly mentioned and repeated. And conſidering, That, if the Corporation

FIFTH WARRANT.

His Majeſty ordained a charter to paſs the Seals of Scotland,

confirming the privileges formerly granted to the Bank;

FIFTH WARRANT.

and further impowering the Governor, &c. with the approbation of a General Court of Proprietors, to transfer the said 111,000 l. of Equivalent Stock.

poration of the said *Royal Bank* had power to assign and transfer the aforesaid One hundred and eleven thousand pounds of Equivalent Stock, they would thereby be enabled to carry on the business of Banking to a greater extent, which would be of great advantage to that part of the united kingdom, and would very much promote the trade, manufactures, and improvements of that country, his Majesty thereby gave and granted full power and authority to the Governor, Deputy-Governor, and Directors of the said Company of *The Royal Bank of Scotland*, by and with the direction and approbation of a General Court of the Proprietors thereof, to assign and transfer the said sum of One hundred and eleven thousand pounds of Equivalent Stock, originally subscribed into the said *Royal Bank*, or such part of it as they should find necessary, to any person or persons, bodies politic

tic and corporate, notwithstanding that the same was incorporated of the Stock of the said *Royal Bank;* and his Majesty thereby declared, That such transfers or assignments should be good, valid, and sufficient to such person or persons, bodies politic and corporate, who should purchase the said Equivalent Stock, or any part thereof. And to remove any doubt as to the subsisting of the said Corporation or Company of *The Royal Bank of Scotland,* after the transferring the said Equivalent Stock, his Majesty thereby declared and directed, that, notwithstanding of such transfers or assignments of the said Equivalent Stock, the said Corporation or Company of *The Royal Bank of Scotland* should and might, after such transfers or assignments, as aforesaid, continue for ever, and have perpetual succession, and enjoy all the privileges, benefits, and advantages whatsoever, given and granted to them

FIFTH WARRANT.

Such transfers to be good and effectual to the purchasers.

The Corporation of the Bank to subsist notwithstanding of such transfers,

and continue to enjoy all the privileges formerly granted to them.

by

FIFTH WARRANT.

by the said two recited charters or letters patent, as if no such transfers or assignments had been made; and from and after the making of such transfers or assignments of the said Equivalent Stock, the monies arising therefrom should be and be deemed part of the Stock of the said Company or Corporation of *The Royal Bank*, and should belong to the Proprietors of the said Bank, in proportion to their shares and interest; and should be assignable or transferable in such and the like manner, *mutatis mutandis*, as the shares in the Capital Stock and yearly Fund are now assignable or might be assigned; and that upon such assigning or transferring of the said sum of One hundred and eleven thousand pounds of Equivalent Stock, or any part thereof, the Proprietors of the said Stock in the said *Royal Bank*, or the majority of them, in a General Court, should and might, and they were thereby impowered

The money arising from the sale of such Equivalent Stock, should be deemed part of the Stock of the Bank,

Transferable in the same manner as the shares in the Capital Stock and yearly fund are now assignable.

The Proprietors might authorise the Court of Directors to receive the monies arising from the sales of said Equivalent Stock.

[251]

powered and authorised to give sufficient authority to their Court of Directors, or such other person or persons as they should please to nominate and appoint, to receive the money that should be paid or payable to the Company or Corporation, upon such transfers or assignments of the said Equivalent Stock; and also that it should and might be lawful to and for the majority of the Proprietors of the said Company and Corporation, present at their General Court or Courts, and they were thereby impowered and authorised to impower their said Court of Directors, from time to time, to lay out and invest the money that should be received for the said Equivalent Stock, or any part thereof, upon such security and securities as the said majority of the said Proprietors in such General Courts should think fit to direct and appoint; and that the interest and produce arising by and from such money, or the securities

FIFTH WARRANT.

The Proprietors may authorise the Court of Directors to lay out such monies upon such securities as they should think fit.

FIFTH
WARRANT.

The intereſt and produce ariſing from ſuch monies to be divideo amongſt the Proprietors, as a General Court ſhould direct.

ſecurities taken for the ſame, ſhould be divided to and amongſt the Proprietors of the Stock of *The Royal Bank*, in ſuch way and manner, and by ſuch methods, as the General Court of the ſaid Company and Corporation, or the majority of them, ſhould direct and determine; and that the ſaid money ſo paid in, and the ſecurities taken for the

The ſaid money, and ſecurities taken for the ſame, to be ſubject to the ſame rules and directions as the then Capital Stock of the Company.

ſame, ſhould be under the direction of the General Courts of the Corporation, and the Governor, Deputy-Governor, and Directors of the ſaid Company or Corporation, in the ſame way and manner, and ſubject to the ſame rules and directions as the preſent Capital Stock of the ſaid Corporation or Company were then under; to the end that a ſure and permanent fund might ſubſiſt for the credit of the ſaid Bank, and ſecurity of ſuch as dealt with them. Provided always, That no dividend ſhould be made to the Proprietors of the ſaid Stock of the

ſaid

said Company, after such assignments or transfers of the said stock, but out of the interest of the money arising from the sale or sales of the said Equivalent Stock, and out of the profit arising and to arise by borrowing and lending of money, and dealing in the trade and business of Banking, as aforesaid. And his Majesty did, for himself, his heirs, and successors, grant and declare, That these his letters patent should be in and by all things valid and effectual in the law, according to the true intent and meaning of the same, and should be taken, construed, and adjudged, in the most favourable and beneficial sense, for the best advantage of the said Corporation, notwithstanding of any misrecital, defaults, uncertainty, or imperfection, in these his Majesty's letters patent, as by the said grant or letters patent, passed under the Seal appointed by the Treaty of Union to be kept in

FIFTH WARRANT.

Dividends should only be made out of the interest of the said monies, and from the profits arising from Banking.

These presents to be construed in the most favourable sense for the advantage of the Corporation.

[254]

FIFTH WARRANT.

in Scotland, in place of the Great Seal thereof, relation being thereunto had, may and doth more fully and at large appear. And whereas by charter or letters patent under the Seal appointed by the Treaty of Union to be kept in Scotland, in place of the Great Seal thereof, and bearing date the tenth day of June one thousand seven hundred and eight-three, reciting to the effect before recited, and also reciting, That, since obtaining the said patents, the said Company had carried on the business of Banking in Scotland much to the benefit of the trade, manufactures, and improvements of that part of the united kingdom, and that they, agreeable to the powers vested in them, by the letters patent of his late most glorious Majesty King George the Second, dated tenth November one thousand seven hundred and thirty-eight, before recited, had, from their calls and profits, added to their Capital

Recital of the petition of The Royal Bank to his Majesty,

That they had carried on the business of Banking to the benefit of trade, &c.:

Capital Stock the sum of Thirty-eight thousand six hundred and fifty-two pounds one penny and seven-twelfths of a penny Sterling, and whereby the same amounted to One hundred and fifty thousand pounds Sterling; and that they would be able to carry the good purposes of their erection on to a higher degree, and with greater benefit to the country, if they were impowered to enlarge their Capital to the extent of One hundred and fifty thousand pounds Sterling more, in the same way or manner, and with such provisions as were contained in the said charter, dated the first of November one thousand seven hundred and thirty-eight: And therefore that they had applied to his Majesty, That he would be graciously pleased, by letters patent under the Great Seal of Scotland, to ratify and confirm their privileges, authorities, and rights formerly granted to them, by the foresaid charter

FIFTH WARRANT.

That it would be highly advantageous to the country were they allowed to enlarge their capital to the extent of 150,000l. more.

Praying his Majesty to confirm their privileges;

FIFTH
WARRANT.

and to impower
the Governor, &c.
with approbation
of a General Court
of Proprietors, to
enlarge their capi-
tal by a sum not ex-
ceeding 150,000l.
by subscriptions of
Equivalent Stock,
land security, &c.

charter erecting *The Royal Bank*, and the said other several before recited letters patent obtained by them; and to authorise and impower the Governor, Deputy-Governor, and Directors of the said *Royal Bank of Scotland*, with the direction and approbation of a General Court of Proprietors, to enlarge their then Capital to any sum not exceeding One hundred and fifty thousand pounds Sterling, so as the Stock might amount in all to Three hundred thousand pounds Sterling; and to make such enlargement by taking in subscriptions of Equivalent Stock, by heritable land securities, or by any other way that the Directors of the said *Royal Bank*, by and with the consent of the said General Court of Proprietors, should judge safe and beneficial to the Bank, in the same way and manner, and with such powers and provisions as were contained in the said charter and letters patent, dated the first day of November

vember one thousand seven hundred and thirty-eight; therefore his Majesty ordained a charter to be made and passed under the Seal appointed by the Treaty of Union to be kept in Scotland, in place of the Great Seal thereof, ratifying and confirming, as his Majesty thereby ratified and confirmed, all the privileges, authorities, and rights formerly granted to the said Company or Corporation of *The Royal Bank of Scotland*, by the said charter or letters patent, bearing date the thirty-first day of May in the year one thousand seven hundred and twenty-seven, erecting the said *Royal Bank*; and by the said letters patent thereafter granted to the said *Bank*, bearing date the first day of November, in the year one thousand seven hundred and thirty-eight; and by the said charter and letters patent, dated the sixteenth day of May one thousand seven hundred and seventy, in as ample man-

K k   ner

FIFTH WARRANT.

His Majesty ordained a charter to pass the Seals of Scotland,

confirming the privileges formerly granted to the Bank;

FIFTH WARRANT.

ner and form, as if the fame had all been particularly mentioned and repeated: And confidering, That the then Capital of the faid Company was not fufficient to anfwer the feveral good purpofes of their erection, and that the addition of a fum to the faid Capital might facilitate their operations, and enable them to be further ufeful to that part of the united kingdom, by carrying on their bufinefs of Banking to a greater extent, and with more fecurity, which would be of great advantage to and much promote the trade, manufactures, and improvements of that country; therefore his Majefty thereby gave full power and authority to the Governor, Deputy-Governor, and Directors of the faid Company of *The Royal Bank of Scotland*, by and with the direction and approbation of a General Court of the Proprietors thereof, to enlarge their then Capital of One hundred and fifty thoufand

and authorifing the Governor, Deputy-Governor, & Directors of the faid Company, with approbation of a General Court of Proprietors, to enlarge their capital to any fum not exceeding 300,000l.

thousand pounds Sterling, to any sum not exceeding Three hundred thousand pounds Sterling in the whole; and that either by taking subscriptions of other Equivalent Stock, not then subscribed into the said Bank, or by taking in subscriptions of certain sums of money upon land security, or any other ways and means that the said Directors of *The Royal Bank of Scotland*, by the consent of the said General Court of the Proprietors, should judge most safe and beneficial to the Corporation of the said *Royal Bank*; and to that end, his Majesty authorised and impowered the said Directors to take and receive such subscriptions, in such way and manner as the General Court of the said Proprietors should direct: And for completing the said additional stock of One hundred and fifty thousand pounds Sterling, it should and might be lawful to and for the Proprietors of

FIFTH WARRANT.

The Directors to receive subscriptions in such way as the General Court of Proprietors should direct,

for completing the additional stock of 150,000 l.

FIFTH
WARRANT.

of the said Company of *The Royal Bank*, or the majority of them, in any General Court of the said Company, to be held as in the former charter was mentioned and directed, either to allow the Proprietors of such part of the Equivalent Stock, to subscribe such further or other part of the stock of the said Company into the stock of the said Company of *The Royal Bank*, not exceeding in whole the sum of One hundred and fifty thousand pounds, upon such terms and conditions, and at such times as the majority of the Proprietors of *The Royal Bank of Scotland* in such General Courts should limit and appoint; or it should and might be lawful for the majority of the Proprietors of the said *Royal Bank of Scotland* to take in such additional stock of One hundred and fifty thousand pounds Sterling, by a voluntary subscription, either of money upon heritable security or otherwise,

[margin notes:]
To allow the Proprietors of Equivalent Stock to subscribe such part of the Stock of the said Company into the Stock of *The Royal Bank*, not exceeding 150,000 l.;

or to take such additional stock by a voluntary subscription, either of money, heritable security, or otherwise.

wife, and upon such terms and conditions, and at such times, as the majority of the Proprietors of the said Company, in such General Court, should limit, direct, and appoint. And his Majesty declared and directed, That such stock of *The Equivalent Company*, so to be subscribed in the terms aforesaid, and such subscriptions so to be made in money upon heritable security or otherwise, should, from and after such subscription, be under the management, care, and direction of the said Corporation or Company of *The Royal Bank*, from the time of such subscription, in the same way and manner as the stock formerly subscribed was, by the said former charters or letters patent, directed and appointed; and that the same, and the Proprietors, subscribers thereof, should and might, upon the terms and conditions so to be limited and appointed, from the time of such subscription as aforesaid,

FIFTH WARRANT.

The stock so subscribed, &c. to be under the direction of the Corporation of *The Royal Bank*, as the stock formerly subscribed.

To have the same privileges as the Proprietors of the first subscribed stock.

FIFTH WARRANT.

Transferable in the same way therewith.

said, have all the same privileges and liberties as the Proprietors of the first subscribed stock, and proportions thereof, should have and enjoy; and that such new stock, so to be subscribed, should be transferable in the same way and manner, and upon the same terms and conditions, as the then present stock of the said Company was then transferable, by virtue of or under the said charter of the thirty-first day of May, in the year one thousand seven hundred and twenty-seven; and charter dated the first day of November one thousand seven hundred and thirty-eight; and charter dated the sixteenth day of May one thousand seven hundred and seventy; and the Proprietors of such subscribed stock should be entitled to have and receive the same, or the like dividends, as should from time to time be declared upon the then present Capital of the said Corporation or Company. And his Majesty declared

and

and directed, That, in case the Parliament of Great Britain should, at any time or times, think proper to redeem the said Equivalent Stock, or such part thereof as had been or should be subscribed into the said Company of *The Royal Bank of Scotland*, or that the said Company should assign or transfer the same as aforesaid, yet, that the said Corporation or Company of *The Royal Bank of Scotland*, notwithstanding thereof, should and might, after such redemption or transfer, continue for ever, and have perpetual succession, and enjoy all the privileges, benefits, and advantages whatsoever, given and granted to them by the said recited charters or letters patent, except the share or interest in the said annual fund of Ten thousand pounds, as aforesaid, as if no such redemption or transfer were had or made; and from and after such redemption or transfer, all persons having any share

or

marginalia:
FIFTH WARRANT.

Notwithstanding the Parliament should redeem the Equivalent Stock, the Corporation of *The Royal Bank* should still continue;

and enjoy all former privileges, except the share in the annual fund of 10,000l.

FIFTH WARRANT.	
After redemption, all perfons having intereft or ftock paid into or gained by the Company, to carry on the trade of the Company, fhould be deemed Members, and entitled to all advantages thereof;	or intereft, or ftock paid into or gained by the faid Company, to carry on the trade of the faid Company, fhould be and be deemed Members of the faid Company, and be entitled to all the benefits, privileges, and advantages thereof, in proportion to their refpective fhares and interefts in the faid money or ftock as aforefaid; and
and the ftock fo paid, or to be paid, fhould be transferable, in like manner as the fhares in the Capital Stock and yearly fund were then affignable.	the faid money or ftock fo paid, or to be paid, fhould be affignable or tranfferable in fuch and the like manner, *mutatis mutandis*, as the faid fhares in the Capital Stock and yearly fund were then affignable or might be affigned; and
The Proprietors in a General Court, or majority of them, impowered to give fufficient authority to their Court of Directors, or fuch perfons as they fhould nominate, to receive the money payable to the Company upon fuch redemption as aforefaid, and difcharge the fame.	that, upon fuch redemption or transfer as aforefaid, the Proprietors of the faid ftock in the faid *Royal Bank*, or the majority of them in a General Court, fhould and might, and they were thereby impowered and authorifed to give fufficient authority to their Court of Directors, or fuch other perfon or perfons as they fhould nominate and

[265]

and appoint, to receive the money that should be paid or payable to the Company or Corporation, upon such redemption or transfers, and give receipts, acquittances, or discharges for the same; and also, That it should and might be lawful to and for the majority of the said Proprietors, present at their General Court or Courts, to impower their said Court of Directors, from time to time, to lay out and invest the money that should, upon such redemption or transfer, be paid as aforesaid, upon such security and securities as the said majority of the Proprietors in such General Court should think fit to direct and appoint; and that the interest and produce arising by and from such money, or the securities taken for the same, should be divided to and among the Proprietors of the stock of *The Royal Bank*, in such way and manner, and by such methods, as the General Court

FIFTH WARRANT.

The Proprietors might authorise the Court of Directors to lay out such monies upon such securities as they should think fit.

The interest and produce arising from such monies to be divided amongst the Proprietors, as a General Court should direct.

of

FIFTH
WARRANT.

The said money, and securities taken for the same, to be subject to the same rules and directions as the then Capital Stock of the Company.

Dividends should only be made out of the interest of the said monies, and from the profits arising from Banking.

of the said Company, or the majority of them, should direct and determine; and that the said money so paid in, and the securities taken for the same, should be under the direction of the General Courts of the Corporation, and the Governor, Deputy-Governor, and Directors of the said Company or Corporation, in the same way and manner, and subject to the same directions and authorities as the then present Capital Stock of the said Corporation or Company were under. Provided always, That no dividend should be made to the Proprietors of the said stock of the said Company, after such redemption or transfer as aforesaid, but out of the interest of money payable to them, upon such redemption or transfer as aforesaid, and out of the profit arising and to arise by borrowing and lending of money, and dealing in the trade and business of Banking, as aforesaid. And his

his Majesty did, for himself, his heirs, and successors, grant and declare, That his said letters patent should be in and by all things valid and effectual in the law, according to the true intent and meaning of the same, and should be taken, construed, and adjudged, in the most favourable and beneficial sense, for the best advantage of the said Corporation, notwithstanding of any misrecital, defaults, uncertainty, or imperfection, in his Majesty's said letters patent, as by the said grant or letters patent, passed under the Seal appointed by the Treaty of Union to be kept in Scotland, in place of the Great Seal thereof, relation being thereunto had, may and doth more fully and at large appear. And our Sovereign Lord considering, That the Governor, Deputy-Governor, and Directors of the said *Royal Bank of Scotland*, have, by their most humble application to his Majesty, under their Seal, represented, That,

FIFTH WARRANT.

These presents to be construed in the most favourable sense for the advantage of the Corporation.

Recital of the petition of *The Royal Bank* to his Majesty,

[268]

FIFTH WARRANT.

That they have carried on the bufinefs of Banking to the benefit of trade, &c.:

That it would be highly advantageous to the country were they allowed to enlarge their capital to the extent of 300,000l. more.

That, fince obtaining the faid letters patent laft above recited, the faid *Royal Bank* have been enabled, from the favings made by them fince the erection of the Bank, to increafe their Capital Stock to Three hundred thoufand pounds Sterling, without opening further fubfcriptions, or making any calls whatever upon the Proprietors of the Bank, and have thereby been enabled to carry on the bufinefs of Banking in Scotland much to the benefit of the trade, manufactures, and improvements of that part of the united kingdom, and that they are convinced that they would be able to carry on the good purpofes of their erection to a ftill higher degree, and with greater benefit to the trade, manufactures, and improvements of the country, if they were impowered to enlarge their prefent Capital to the extent of Three hundred thoufand pounds Sterling more, in the fame way and manner, and with such provisions as are contained in the last mentioned letters patent, bearing date the tenth day of June in the year one thousand seven hundred and eighty-three; and have therefore prayed his Majesty, That he would be graciously pleased, by letters patent under the Great Seal of Scotland, to ratify and confirm the privileges, authorities, and rights granted to them, by the foresaid charter erecting *The Royal Bank*, and the several letters patent herein above recited; and to authorise and impower them, and their successors in office, with the direction and approbation of a General Court of Proprietors, to enlarge their present Capital Stock by any further sum not exceeding Three hundred thousand pounds Sterling, so as the stock may amount in all to Six hundred thousand pounds Sterling; and to make such enlargement by taking in subscriptions of Equivalent Stock, by heritable

FIFTH WARRANT.

Praying his Majesty to confirm their privileges;

and to impower the Governor, &c. with approbation of a General Court of Proprietors, to enlarge their Capital by a sum not exceeding 300,000l. by subscriptions of Equivalent Stock, land security, &c.

FIFTH WARRANT.

able land fecurities, or by any other way that the Governor, Deputy-Governor, and Directors of the faid Bank, by and with confent of a General Court of Proprietors, fhould judge fafe and beneficial to the Bank, in the fame way and manner, and with fuch powers and provifions as are contained in the faid letters patent and charter herein laft above recited.

The petition referred to his Majefty's Advocate for Scotland;

And confidering, That fuch petition has been referred to his Majefty's Advocate for Scotland for his opinion, what might be reafonable and fitting for his Majefty to do therein; and his Majefty having taken into his

and the fame, with his faid Advocate's report thereon, being taken into confideration,

royal confideration the faid petition, and the report thereupon made by his faid Advocate, and being willing to give all proper encouragement to fuch an undertaking; therefore his Majefty, in compliance with the faid requeft, and by virtue of his prerogative royal, and of his efpecial grace,

certain

certain knowledge, and mere motion, ordains a charter to be made and paſſed under the Seal appointed by the Treaty of Union to be kept in Scotland, in place of the Great Seal thereof, ratifying and confirming, as his Majeſty does hereby ratify and confirm, all the privileges, authorities, and rights formerly granted to the ſaid Company or Corporation of *The Royal Bank of Scotland*, by the ſaid charter or letters patent, bearing date the thirty-firſt day of May in the year one thouſand ſeven hundred and twenty-ſeven, erecting the ſaid *Royal Bank;* and by the ſaid letters patent thereafter granted to the ſaid Bank, bearing date the firſt day of November, in the year one thouſand ſeven hundred and thirty-eight; and by the ſaid charter and letters patent, dated the ſixteenth day of May one thouſand ſeven hundred and ſeventy; and by the ſaid letters patent, dated the tenth day of June,

marginalia: FIFTH WARRANT. his Majeſty ordains a charter to paſs the Seals of Scotland, confirming the privileges formerly granted to the Bank;

FIFTH
WARRANT.

June, in the year one thousand seven hundred and eighty-three, in as ample manner and form, as if the same were all herein particularly mentioned and repeated: And to the end that the said *Royal Bank of Scotland* may be the better encouraged to proceed in the laudable undertaking of Banking, so much for the benefit of the subjects in that part of the united kingdom; and considering, That the present Capital Stock of the said Company of *The Royal Bank of Scotland* is not sufficient to answer the several good purposes of their erection, and that the addition of a sum to their present Capital may facilitate their operations, and enable them to be further useful to that part of the united kingdom, by carrying on their business of Banking to a greater extent, and with more security, which would be of great advantage to and much promote the trade, manufactures, and improvements of

that

that country; therefore his Majesty hereby gives full power and authority to the Governor, Deputy-Governor, and Directors of the said Company of *The Royal Bank of Scotland*, by and with the direction and approbation of a General Court of the Proprietors thereof, to enlarge their present Capital of Three hundred thousand pounds Sterling, to any sum not exceeding Six hundred thousand pounds Sterling in the whole; and that either by taking subscriptions of other Equivalent Stock, not already subscribed into the said Bank, or by taking in subscriptions of certain sums of money upon land security, or any other ways and means that the said Directors of *The Royal Bank of Scotland*, by the consent of the said General Court of the Proprietors, shall judge most safe and beneficial to the Corporation of the said *Royal Bank*; and to that end, his Majesty does,

FIFTH WARRANT, and authorising the Governor, Deputy-Governor, & Directors of the said Company, with approbation of a General Court of Proprietors, to enlarge their capital to any sum not exceeding 600,000l.

[274]

FIFTH
WARRANT.

The Directors to receive subscriptions in such way as the General Court of Proprietors shall direct,

for completing the additional stock of 300,000 l.

To allow the Proprietors of Equivalent Stock to subscribe such part of the Stock of the said Company into the Stock of *The Royal Bank*, not exceeding 300,000 l.;

does, by these presents, authorise and impower the said Directors to take and receive such subscriptions, in such way and manner as the General Court of the said Proprietors shall direct: And for completing the said additional stock of Three hundred thousand pounds Sterling, it shall and may be lawful to and for the Proprietors of the said Company of *The Royal Bank*, or the majority of them, in any General Court of the said Company, to be held as in the said former charter is mentioned and directed, either to allow the Proprietors of such part of the Equivalent Stock, to subscribe such further or other part of the stock of the said Company into the stock of the said Company of *The Royal Bank*, not exceeding in the whole the sum of Three hundred thousand pounds, upon such terms and conditions, and at such times as the majority of the Proprietors of *The Royal Bank of Scotland*

Scotland in fuch General Courts fhall limit and appoint; or it fhall and may be lawful for the majority of the Proprietors of the faid *Royal Bank of Scotland* to take in fuch additional ftock of Three hundred thoufand pounds Sterling, by a voluntary fubfcription, either of money upon heritable fecurity or otherwife, and upon fuch terms and conditions, and at fuch times, as the majority of the Proprietors of the faid Company of *The Royal Bank of Scotland*, in fuch General Court, fhall limit, direct, and appoint. And his Majefty doth hereby declare and direct, That fuch ftock of *The Equivalent Company*, fo to be fubfcribed in the terms aforefaid, and fuch fubfcriptions fo to be made in money upon heritable fecurity or otherwife, fhall, from and after fuch fubfcription, be under the management, care, and direction of the Corporation or Company of *The Royal Bank,*

FIFTH WARRANT.

or to take fuch additional ftock by a voluntary fubfcription, either of money, heritable fecurity, or otherwife.

The ftock fo fubfcribed, &c. to be under the direction of the Corporation of *The Royal Bank*, as the ftock formerly fubfcribed.

FIFTH
WARRANT.

To have the same privileges as the Proprietors of the first subscribed stock.

Transferable in the same way therewith.

Bank, from the time of such subscription, in the same way and manner as the stock formerly subscribed was, by the said former charters or letters patent, directed and appointed; and that the same, and the Proprietors, subscribers thereof, shall and may, upon the terms and conditions so to be limited and appointed, from the time of such subscription as aforesaid, have all the same privileges and liberties as the Proprietors of the first subscribed stock, and proportions thereof, shall have and enjoy; and that such new stock, so to be subscribed, shall be transferable in the same way and manner, and upon the same terms and conditions, as the present stock of the said Company is now transferable, by virtue of or under the said charter of the thirty-first day of May, in the year one thousand seven hundred and twenty-seven; and charter dated the first day of November one thousand

FIFTH WARRANT.

thoufand feven hundred and thirty-eight; and charter dated the fixteenth day of May one thoufand feven hundred and feventy; and charter dated the tenth day of June one thoufand feven hundred and eighty-three; and the Proprietors of fuch fubfcribed ftock fhall be entitled to have and receive the fame, or the like dividends, as fhall from time to time be declared upon the prefent Capital of the faid Corporation or Company. And his Majefty, for the better encouragement of the faid *Royal Bank* to proceed in and continue their undertaking of Banking, fo much for the benefit of the fubjects of that part of his united kingdom, declares and directs, That, in cafe the Parliament of Great Britain fhall, at any time or times, think proper to redeem the faid Equivalent Stock, or fuch part thereof as has been or fhall be fubfcribed into the faid Company of *The Royal*

Notwithftanding the Parliament fhould redeem the Equivalent Stock, the Corporation of *The Royal Bank* fhall ftill continue;

FIFTH WARRANT.

Royal Bank of Scotland, or that the said Corporation or Company of *The Royal Bank of Scotland* shall assign or transfer the same as aforesaid, yet, that the said Corporation or Company of *The Royal Bank of Scotland*, notwithstanding thereof, shall and may, after such redemption or transfer as aforesaid, continue for ever, and have perpetual succession, and enjoy all the privileges, benefits, and advantages whatever, given and granted to them by the said recited charters or letters patent,

and enjoy all former privileges, except the share in the annual fund of 10,000l.

except the share or interest in the said annual fund of Ten thousand pounds, as aforesaid, as if no such redemption or transfer were had or made; and

After redemption, all persons having interest or stock paid into or gained by the Company, to carry on the trade of the Company, shall be deemed Members, and entitled to all advantages thereof;

from and after such redemption or transfer, all persons having any share or interest, or stock paid into or gained by the said Company, to carry on the trade of the said Company, shall be and be deemed Members of the said Company, and be entitled

to

to all the benefits, privileges, and advantages thereof, in proportion to their respective shares and interests in the said money or stock as aforesaid; and the said money or stock so paid, or to be paid, shall be assignable or transferable in such and the like manner, *mutatis mutandis*, as the said shares in the Capital Stock and yearly fund are now assignable or may be assigned; and that, upon such redemption or transfer as aforesaid, the Proprietors of the said stock in the said *Royal Bank*, or the majority of them in a General Court, shall and may, and they are hereby impowered and authorised to give sufficient authority to their Court of Directors, or such other person or persons as they shall please to nominate and appoint, to receive the money that shall be paid or payable to the Company or Corporation, upon such redemption or transfer as aforesaid, and give receipts, acquittances, or discharges

FIFTH WARRANT.

and the stock so paid, or to be paid, shall be transferable, in like manner as the shares in the Capital Stock and yearly fund are now assignable.

The Proprietors in a General Court, or majority of them, impowered to give sufficient authority to their Court of Directors, or such persons as they shall nominate, to receive the money payable to the Company upon such redemption as aforesaid, and discharge the same.

FIFTH WARRANT.

The Proprietors may authorife the Court of Directors to lay out fuch monies upon fuch fecurities as they fhall think fit.

charges for the fame; and alfo, That it fhall and may be lawful to and for the majority of the faid Proprietors of the faid Company and Corporation, prefent at their General Court or Courts, and they are hereby impowered and authorifed to impower their faid Court of Directors, from time to time, to lay out and inveft the money that fhall, upon fuch redemption or tranffer, be paid as aforefaid, upon fuch fecurity and fecurities as the faid majority of the Proprietors in fuch General Court fhall think fit to direct and appoint;

The intereft and produce arifing from fuch monies to be divided amongft the Proprietors, as a General Court fhall direct.

and that the intereft and produce arifing by and from fuch money, or the fecurities taken for the fame, fhall be divided to and amongft the Proprietors of the ftock of *The Royal Bank*, in fuch way and manner, and by fuch methods, as the General Court of the faid Company or Corporation, or the majority of them, fhall direct and determine; and that the faid money fo paid in, in, and the securities taken for the same, shall be under the direction of the General Courts of the Corporation, and the Governor, Deputy-Governor, and Directors of the said Company or Corporation, in the same way and manner, and subject to the same directions and authorities as the present Capital Stock of the said Corporation or Company are now under; to the end that a sure and permanent fund may subsist for the credit of the said Bank, and security of such as deal with them. Provided always, That no dividend shall be made to the Proprietors of the said stock of the said Company, after such redemption or transfer as aforesaid, but out of the interest of money payable to them, upon such redemption or transfer as aforesaid, and out of the profits arising and to arise by borrowing and lending of money, and dealing in the trade and business of Banking, as aforesaid. And

FIFTH WARRANT.

The said money, and securities taken for the same, to be subject to the same rules and directions as the present Capital Stock of the Company.

Dividends shall only be made out of the interest of the said monies, and from the profits arising from Banking.

FIFTH
WARRANT.

These presents to
be construed in the
most favourable
sense for the advan-
tage of the Corpo-
ration.

His Majesty cove-
nants to give such
further privileges
as he may lawfully
grant;

his Majesty doth, for himself, his heirs, and successors, grant and declare, That those his letters patent shall be in and by all things valid and sufficient in the law, according to the true intent and meaning of the same, and shall be taken, construed, and adjudged, in the most favourable and beneficial sense, for the best advantage of the said Corporation, notwithstanding any misrecital, defaults, uncertainty, or imperfection, in those his Majesty's letters patent. And his Majesty doth hereby, for himself, his heirs, and successors, covenant, grant, and agree to and with the said Corporation or Body Politic, and their successors, That he, his heirs, and successors, shall and will, from time to time, and at all times hereafter, upon the humble suit and request of the said Corporation or Body Politic, and their successors, give and grant unto them all such further and other privileges, authorities, matters,

ters, and things, for rendering more effectual this his grant, according to the true intent and meaning of these presents, which he or they can and may lawfully grant, and as shall be reasonably advised and devised by the counsel learned in the law of the said Corporation or Body Politic for the time being, and shall be approved of by the Advocate or Solicitor General for Scotland of his Majesty, his heirs, and successors, on his or their behalf. And his Majesty doth further will and command, That the said Charter do pass the said Seal appointed to be kept and used in Scotland in place of the Great Seal *per saltum*, without passing any other seal or register. For doing whereof, this shall be, as well to the Director of his Majesty's Chancery in Scotland for writing the same, as to the Keeper of the said Seal for causing the said Seal to be appended thereto, a sufficient warrant.—Given at our Court at

FIFTH WARRANT.

which shall be devised by their own counsel, and approved of by the Lord Advocate or Solicitor General for Scotland for the time.

FIFTH
WARRANT.
at St James's this fifth day of June one thoufand feven hundred and eighty-eight, in the twenty-eight year of our reign.

www.ingramcontent.com/pod-product-compliance
Lightning Source LLC
Chambersburg PA
CBHW032106220426
43664CB00008B/1147